The Imperial Temptation

The Imperial Temptation

The New World Order and America's Purpose

ROBERT W. TUCKER
DAVID C. HENDRICKSON

COUNCIL ON FOREIGN RELATIONS PRESS

NEW YORK

COUNCIL ON FOREIGN RELATIONS BOOKS

If you would like more information on Council publications, please write the Council on Foreign Relations, 58 East 68th Street, New York, NY 10021, or call the Publications Office at (212)734-0400.

Library of Congress Cataloging-in-Publication Data

Tucker, Robert W.
    The imperial temptation : the new world order and America's
purpose / by Robert Tucker and David Hendrickson.
        p.   cm.
    Includes bibliographical references and index.
    ISBN 0-87609-118-4 : $22.50.—ISBN 0-87609-116-8 : $14.95
    1. United States—Foreign relations—1989– 2. Persian Gulf War,
1991.   3. World politics—1985–1995.   I. Hendrickson, David C.
II. Title.
E881.H46   1992
327.73—dc20   92-4155
                                                           CIP

92   93   94   95   96   97   EB   10   9   8   7   6   5   4   3   2   1

Designed by KHTP Design

For Timothy Fuller

CONTENTS

ACKNOWLEDGMENTS

We would like to thank the Council on Foreign Relations for affording us the opportunity of pursuing this work as Whitney H. Shepardson fellows in 1991–1992. The study group, ably organized by Nicholas X. Rizopoulos and chaired by Peter Tarnoff, was of great utility in revising the work. We wish to thank both men for their generous help, as well as to thank the study group participants for their often critical but valuable advice. Helpful research assistance was provided by Michael J. Shaver and Robin Satterwhite. The diligence and editorial expertise of David Kellogg, David Haproff, Judy Train, Anu Ponnamma, and Liz Cunningham of the Council's publications division are also appreciated. Thanks are due, as always, to Judith and Clelia, for their forbearance during the composition of the book, and to Katherine, Wesley, and Whitney, for general inspiration.

Robert W. Tucker
Santa Fe, New Mexico

David C. Hendrickson
Colorado Springs, Colorado

January 1992

INTRODUCTION

Two Victories

I n 1989, a great conflict that had persisted for more than four decades, and that was expected to continue for decades to come, suddenly ended in a victory that was as sweeping as it was unexpected. Change that is normally associated only with the outcome of a major war was attended by the virtual absence of armed conflict. In the long history of great power conflicts, there has seldom, if ever, been so remarkable a victory as that resulting from the Soviet Union's withdrawal from its long-held position in central and eastern Europe without obtaining anything approximating a quid pro quo from its adversaries.

In the United States, however, the end of the cold war evoked a curiously subdued reaction. While a sense of accomplishment and relief was apparent, it was uncharacteristically restrained. The same was true of the triumphant mood that emerged in this period. Clearly, the end of the cold war did not provoke anything comparable to the outburst of national pride that marked the military defeat of Iraq in 1991, despite the consideration that there was no realistic comparison between the two victories, just as there was no realistic comparison between the threats to American interests posed by the Soviet Union and Iraq.

The disparity between the nation's reaction to the end of the cold war and the military defeat of Iraq is striking, for the response to each event appears almost inversely proportionate to its significance. In 1990, the American government could respond to Iraq's invasion of Kuwait with measures it would have shrunk from taking in the circumstances of a decade earlier. It could do so

1

2   because its relationship with the Soviet Union had since been transformed almost beyond recognition. Whereas a decade earlier, U.S. military intervention in the Persian Gulf would have entailed a serious risk of conflict with the Soviet Union, in 1990 that risk could be safely excluded. The passing of the cold war made the war against Iraq possible. Without the former event, there would have been no international coalition led by the United States and acting under authority of the United Nations, just as there would not have been anywhere near the support for military action against Iraq from our major allies. In a broader perspective, the victory over Iraq was made possible above all by the far greater victory over the Soviet Union that preceded it.

★   ★   ★

The end of the cold war had dramatically broadened the area of freedom for the nation's foreign policy. For many, it promised a return to the traditional order of things in which domestic policy would regain the primacy it had lost during a half-century of war and cold war. Though threats to the nation's security still had to be anticipated in the post–cold war world, the seriousness of these threats seemed certain to be different from the threats of the last fifty years. Previously the threats had emanated from hostile great powers and encompassed not only a military but an ideological dimension. Following the cold war, the prospective military threats were those of middle or small powers, and no viable ideological challenges were discernible. The great threats to the nation's security—whether physical or ideological—had come to an end with the passing of the cold war. With that close, it seemed reasonable to assume that foreign policy—or at least the conventional security dimension of foreign policy—would assume a more modest and traditional role in the nation's life.

Yet it was not so much a desire to revert to a past order of things that seemed to characterize the national mood on the morrow of victory in the cold war as it was a sense of uncertainty. The cold war may have been won, but what did victory hold out for the American future? If a new order was to succeed the old order of containment and cold war, what was to be its character? In a world in which the totalitarian challenge had so visibly failed and in which the institutions of freedom appeared almost everywhere ascendant, would the United States still be needed as freedom's great champion and defender? And if we were no longer so needed, would we continue to have a distinctive role?

A concern over role is, in itself, scarcely novel. The same concern marked the years preceding the end of the cold war and went hand in hand with the resurgent nationalism of the 1980s. Then it had been in response to a lost war and to a need to redeem a generation marked by a sense of defeat and contrition. A re-affirmation of role had been one means of satisfying this need, and it found its principal expression in the Reagan Doctrine. The Reagan Doctrine cast the nation in the role of *extending* freedom, not merely, as the Truman Doctrine had done, of defending it. Directed, in the president's words, against tyranny "in whatever form, whether of the left or the right," it was against Marxist-Leninist governments that the more direct and serious forms of intervention were pledged. But the sudden end of the cold war made the Reagan Doctrine seem almost irrelevant. The assumption on which it was based—that there was a rising tide of freedom in the world the United States must support—had apparently been borne out to an extent the Doctrine's architects could scarcely have imagined at the time of its conception. That rising tide now threatened to engulf not so much communism's third world periphery as the center itself. If it did, there would no longer be need for either a Truman or a Reagan Doctrine or, for that matter, a nation committed to the role of freedom's defender.

The end of the cold war thus evoked renewed speculation and debate over the role the United States would henceforth play in the world. It also gave rise to a growing debate over policy itself. A change in role could not be considered apart from a change in policy. Sooner or later, the latter had to reflect the former. If the nation's role was no longer that of freedom's champion and de-fender against totalitarianism, its policy would eventually have to change accordingly. But the nature and direction of the change remained uncertain. The policy of containment had been the principal foreign policy of the United States for over forty years. It had remained the center of gravity for American foreign policy

4   despite the criticism and dissatisfaction it engendered and despite the fact that it had been all but disavowed in name—though only in name—by administrations since the late 1960s. The unpopularity of containment notwithstanding, the postwar international order was an order inseparable from containment.

The major institutional expression of containment was the Western Alliance. The direction and management of the alliance constituted the vital center of foreign policy. All else formed the periphery. Although it was the periphery that regularly gave rise to the more intractable and controverted of foreign policy issues—Vietnam being the outstanding example—America's postwar policy had been Eurocentric. It was in Europe that the cold war began just as it was primarily in Europe that the cold war had been waged. The sudden decline of Soviet power and influence that attended the abandonment of its empire in Eastern Europe suddenly deprived the Western Alliance of its principal foundation.

To these uncertainties over role and policy must be added the unease that arose in the United States during the late 1980s over its future international position. Were we destined to lose, and within a relatively brief compass, our preeminent position in the world? The question was asked insistently during the 1980s, largely as a result of the relative weakening of the nation's international economic position. The critical issue in the controversy was whether this development was the inescapable consequence of the global role that America had exercised since World War II—though in ever less favorable circumstances—or whether it was a development that might be arrested and even reversed with the proper remedial policies. However uncertain the answer, the fact that the question was raised at all was significant. The response to what soon came to be known as the "declinist" view indicated that a very sensitive nerve had been touched. Having once experienced a position of world leadership, nothing seemed quite as upsetting as the prospect of losing that position. Nor was this reaction in the least affected by the fact that during the 1980s the Reagan administration had transformed what had been a mere disposition not to pay for the American position in the world into an almost fixed resolve not to do so. Evidently no contradiction

was seen between this resolve and the fervent rejection of a future
in which the United States had lost its position of primacy.

This sensitivity to the prospect of a more modest future also had to be understood in the light of the nation's distinctive past. The United States had never experienced what other nations experienced in achieving a position of world power. It moved within a very brief period from a position of isolation to one of global leadership; it has never been a mere nation among nations. Then, too, the role it had seen itself as playing from infancy, that of freedom's exemplar and savior, reinforced the conviction of a fate set apart from the fate that had overtaken others. Nothing seemed quite as unsettling, even repugnant, as the suggestion that America might instead soon share a fate common to past great powers. Nor was the sting lessened by the realization that a major cause of America's decline might well be the result of the very triumph of America's ideals—the successful engrafting of representative institutions and market systems among our former enemies in World War II.

The sudden end of the cold war did not put an end to the unease over the future of the American position that the declinists had precipitated. If anything, it deepened this unease, for the circumstances surrounding the end of the cold war gave new persuasiveness to the view that the American sun, though still far from setting, had clearly passed its zenith. The decline of the Soviet threat entailed a radical lessening of the security dependence of Western Europe and Japan on the United States. A change in security dependence, however, meant that the essential compact between the protector and the protected, which had held for four decades, no longer held. At the very least, it meant that this compact would no longer hold to anywhere near the extent it had in the past. Henceforth, when significant differences, particularly economic differences, arose between the United States and its major allies, they would no longer be conditioned by the security protection this country extended. A major source of American power and leadership could be relied upon no longer.

In a still broader perspective, the peaceful unfolding of events that in the past would almost surely have been the outcome of war

6   pointed to an international system in the process of profound transformation. The principal features of this transformation were the declining utility of force—above all, in the relations among the major developed states—and the increasing importance of economic power. Even if the American economic position had not declined relative to its major allies, America's power would be diminished in a world in which economic power gradually displaced military power as the *ultima ratio* of state relations. In a number of critical respects the American economic position clearly had declined relative to its major allies, and there was little evidence that this decline might soon be arrested, let alone reversed. The prospect that economic power would increasingly displace military power in the post–cold war system, when combined with the dramatically improved security of America's major allies, prompted the fear that in victory a decline in America's global position was all but inevitable.

★ ★ ★

The lessons widely drawn from America's victory in the gulf war contradicted in almost every respect the meaning that had been assigned to the end of the cold war. Whereas the end of the cold war appeared to dramatically broaden the area of freedom for the nation's foreign policy, the gulf war was taken to show that we still lived in the realm of necessity. The end of the cold war promised a return to a traditional order of things in which domestic policy would regain its accustomed primacy; the gulf war, however, indicated that the relative primacy of foreign policy over domestic policy was a matter of circumstance and not of choice.

Whereas the end of the cold war showed the declining utility of military force in the relations of the great developed states, the gulf war was widely taken as a striking refutation of this view or of any suggestion that the role of force in the international system had changed. Although the gulf crisis was not between great powers and, accordingly, conveyed no direct lessons respecting the conflicts that previously had been of prime importance in world politics, the lesson it was seen to teach about the present role of force had no apparent limitations. This lesson was that the utility of military power remained as central to state relations today as in the past. On this view, the lesson suggested by the end of the cold war was effectively countered by what the gulf crisis so plainly taught.

Disagreement over the role of force was not the only critical difference between the outlook the end of the cold war engendered and the view the gulf crisis revived. The end of the cold war prompted the conclusion by many observers that the world was now a much less dangerous place. This conclusion was not universally shared. There were those who believed that the world of the cold war was less dangerous because it represented the known, whereas a post–cold war world held out the unknown. The cold war had settled down into routine patterns of thought and action. The great protagonists increasingly knew what to expect of each other, and though there continued to be surprises they were ever more infrequent. Moreover, because the superpowers had controlled the behavior of allies and clients, the result was a world that was remarkably stable and predictable. By contrast, a world in which the necessities imposed by the cold war and the controls once exercised by the superpowers were no longer operative was a world that might well prove unstable and unpredictable.

If these considerations persuaded some that a world without the cold war was still dangerous, perhaps even more dangerous than the world it had replaced, the prevailing view was otherwise. Even those, mainly conservatives, for whom the proposition that the world is a dangerous place has always been axiomatic and a point of departure for sound thinking about international politics seemed momentarily disoriented in the wake of the climactic events of 1989. The gulf crisis restored an outlook that had been briefly placed in abeyance. Iraq's invasion of Kuwait was seen as indicative of how dangerous the world continued to be. It showed that threats to vital interests and to the very basis of international order would continue to arise unexpectedly. It also demonstrated that the nature and locale of these threats were unpredictable. Iraq's actions drove home the lesson that confronted with a wide spectrum of possible threats which might arise with little warning time, there was no safe alternative to the retention of substantial forces in being. The expectation that in a post–cold war world the

8   nation's military establishment might be sharply reduced would have to be discarded.

The gulf crisis was also taken as a striking demonstration that there was no viable alternative to American leadership in dealing with threats to international peace and stability. Here again, the lessons of the crisis were seen to refute the widespread expectations that had arisen in the wake of the cold war. Of these expectations, none seemed more plausible than the emergence of a multipolar world in place of the passing bipolar order. A highly qualified multipolarity had existed before the end of the cold war, but this multipolarity had to be understood within the broader context of a persisting bipolarity. Although Germany and Japan were great powers when judged by their economic productivity, their trade balances, and their financial surpluses, they could scarcely be considered so when judged by their security dependence on the United States. The events of the late 1980s, however, put an end to this dependence, which had imposed substantial constraints on their freedom of action in foreign policy. Consequently, it seemed reasonable to expect that the political impact of their economic power would no longer be qualified as it had been during the cold war.

The expectation that a multipolar world would emerge in the wake of the cold war was predicated largely on the assumption that the role of force in world politics had markedly declined. Without that assumption, there was little reason to project the advent of a multipolar world. If military power in the new world was to play essentially the same role and to have the same salience that it had in the old world, then clearly the collapse of Soviet power and influence foreshadowed a period of American hegemony, a period in which American power would overshadow that of all other states in a way it had not done even in the years immediately following World War II. The view that the post–cold war world would not find an America so situated necessarily assumed that economic power, in the form of financial and trade surpluses, would largely displace military power as the *ultima ratio* of state intercourse. By this measure the power of Japan and Germany was

already considerable and promised to become ever more so relative   **9**
to the United States.

   The gulf crisis, though, was widely seen in the United States
as dealing a serious, even fatal, blow to this vision of an emerging
multipolar world. It did so, the prevailing view held, by demonstrating that military power remains as significant as ever in the
relations of states. That the crisis had not involved major powers,
and had instead pitted the world's greatest military power against a
medium-size developing state, was not found to detract from the
lesson presumably taught regarding the continued utility of force.
On the contrary, the gulf war served to persuade most of the nation
of this continued utility as few events have done in the past
generation. It also persuaded many that while American power
remains as dominant as ever, and in some respects even more
dominant than before, the states—Germany and Japan—held up
as the challengers of American dominance remain as dependent as
ever on American military power. The confident expectation that
economic power would displace military power as the principal
measure of influence had been shown to be unfounded. As one
critic of the multipolar vision has written, "The notion that
economic power inevitably translates into geopolitical influence is
a materialist illusion. Economic power is a necessary condition for
great power status. But it certainly is not sufficient, as had been
made clear by the recent behavior of Germany and Japan, which
have generally hidden under the table since the first shots rang out
in Kuwait." [1]

   Thus the world revealed by the gulf crisis is one that remains
very much in need of order; it is also a world that cannot be ordered
today, as it could not be ordered yesterday, by economic power.
Despite the expectations generated by the end of the cold war,
military power remains as indispensable as ever to international
order. The United States alone has both the means and the will to
preserve order in a world that continues to betray as much continuity as change. Yet it also has the interest in assuming a burden
that it alone can presently shoulder. The United States could not
isolate itself from a world that had lapsed into disorder if for no
other reason than the increasing availability of weapons of mass

10   destruction. Saddam Hussein's Iraq provided an impressive demonstration of the implications nuclear proliferation entails for
international order and the nation's security. Whereas the end of
the cold war indicated that the specter of a nuclear holocaust had
sharply receded, the gulf crisis quickly revived nuclear fears, lend-
ing a new sense of urgency to efforts to stop nuclear proliferation
and providing what was for some the most important motive for
the war against Iraq. If this danger, and others as well, are to be
effectively met, the United States has no alternative to a role that
the passing of the cold war was mistakenly seen to have made
irrelevant.

★   ★   ★

Whatever judgment is reached about the validity of these "lessons," it seems likely that they will dominate the debate over
American foreign policy for many years. Just as the "lessons of
Munich" formed the constant reference point for the architects of
American foreign policy in the aftermath of World War II, and as
the contrary "lessons of Vietnam" exercised a no less compelling
hold on the public imagination in the 1970s and 1980s, so the
lessons drawn from the two great world events at the outset of the
1990s seem destined to affect profoundly the way Americans
perceive the role the United States should play in the world.

The lessons drawn from the gulf crisis by many observers rest
on the assumption that it is not change in Europe that reveals the
future but change in the Persian Gulf. The rationale for this
assumption, however, is not apparent, even if the normal order of
things is set aside, and the medium or small powers, rather than
the great powers, are considered to be the prime determinants of
the international system. Assuming, for the sake of argument, that
this is the case, the lessons drawn from the crisis still generalize a
set of circumstances the singularity of which seem, on reflection,
quite clear: There is no other commodity that has the crucial
significance of oil; there is no parallel to the dependence of
developed and developing economies on the energy resources of
the Gulf; these resources are concentrated in an area that remains
relatively inaccessible and highly unstable, and possession of oil

affords an unparalleled financial base whereby an expansionist developing power may hope to realize its aggressive ambitions. These considerations are so apparent that to enumerate them yet again seems redundant. They are enumerated because the sweeping lessons drawn from the gulf crisis largely ignore them.

If, however, the circumstances that attended and largely defined the crisis are not ignored, the more reasonable conclusion is that the gulf crisis is close to being *sui generis*. There is only one Persian Gulf. That fortunate fact must be the point of departure for any sound consideration of the crisis and of the lessons to be drawn from it. The world is not rife with potential Saddam Husseins, for the circumstances that enabled Saddam Hussein to entertain his expansionist designs cannot be readily duplicated. This is so even if the nuclear dimension of the gulf crisis is singled out as its most significant feature because of what it might portend for the international system. Whatever the prospects of nuclear proliferation, one thing seems reasonably clear: the effects of proliferation will not be uniform. Just as the kind of government under which proliferation occurs will make a difference, so will the strategic setting in which proliferation occurs. In terms of the latter, it is difficult to conceive of another setting in the developing world in which proliferation would be more significant, while less desirable, than the Persian Gulf.

These considerations apart, there is no persuasive, nor even plausible, reason for assuming that it is in the Persian Gulf rather than in Europe that the future of international politics is the more clearly revealed. The lessons to be learned from the victorious outcome of the cold war should prove far more significant than the lessons to be learned from the victorious end of the gulf crisis. And while the end of the gulf crisis afforded a striking demonstration of the continued utility of military power when employed by a great state against a small state (especially when such employment is attended by almost ideal political and strategic circumstances), the end of the cold war pointed to the narrowing uses of force in the relations of the great powers. The concluding phase of the cold war demonstrated with startling clarity that if arms continue to

12 serve a vital deterrent function in great power relations, this is the only remaining function they do serve.

In looking back on the 1970s and early 1980s, it is clear that a remarkable event had occurred. An "aspiring second" made its grand bid, saw that bid eventually countered by its adversary, and sensed the prospective decline of its power and influence in the world. The primacy of foreign policy had been axiomatic to the rulers of the Soviet Union for at least a generation. In the name of this primacy Soviet governments had undertaken and justified a massive and sustained arms buildup at great cost and with the avowed objective of an ever expanding world role. Soviet governments not only attached the highest priority to this role, they also received a substantial measure of such domestic legitimacy as they enjoyed from it. Despite some foreign policy successes in the 1970s, by the early 1980s the tide had begun to turn against Moscow. In the principal theaters of contention the Soviet Union's expansionist thrust came to a halt. Although in making the effort Moscow imposed an enormous drain on what was already a chronically ailing economy, the prospect had to be faced of falling further behind the economies of the West.

In the early 1980s, the Soviet leadership must have concluded that the Soviet state was on a rapidly declining path relative to the United States. In the past, such a perception had represented a moment of great danger to the stability of the international system. It did so, for example, in the years prior to World War I when German political opinion became increasingly persuaded that, relative to Great Britain and Russia, German power and influence were on a declining path.

On this most recent occasion, however, a similar perception did not result in war, nor in the serious threat of war. The early 1980s were marked by a Soviet Union that was notably circumspect in its behavior. The revival of the cold war did not give rise to the intense crises that marked the cold war of a generation earlier. In part, the marked restraint shown by Moscow at a time when its strategic position was almost bound to prove a wasting asset may be attributed to an endemic leadership crisis—a crisis that, in turn, reflected the deteriorating condition of the Soviet economy and society. In part, however, this restraint must be seen to support the view that in great power relations the utility of military power has dramatically narrowed. The aggressive and expansionist purposes for which military power could once be used by one great power against another have been progressively deprived of credibility.

The lesson is illustrated by a comparison of two events in the cold war, the Cuban missile crisis and the Euromissile crisis. Separated by a generation and attended by different circumstances in the military position of the parties relative to one another, both events conveyed the same lesson: the difficulty of using military power for other than defensive purposes. In both instances, the Soviet Union sought to use military power, however passively, to alter the status quo to its advantage. In both instances, the attempt failed. That in the first case the United States enjoyed a position of strategic superiority (and in the immediate theater, conventional superiority as well), while in the second it suffered both a strategic and conventional arms disadvantage, made little difference to the successful outcome of each. On both occasions, the Soviet Union proved unwilling to run the risks that were entailed.

Clearly, nothing that occurred in the gulf can detract from the principal lesson of the cold war—that the utility of force in great power relations has been significantly narrowed—for the gulf experience is irrelevant to this lesson. The gulf war did show that in a very different context the utility of force remains less impaired than many had thought, but that lesson should not be confused with the lesson of the cold war.

Nor did the gulf experience fundamentally affect the argument over whether America is in decline. The case of the declinists had centered on the accumulating evidence of serious economic and social ills within the United States. It assumed, as Paul Kennedy put it, that decline was inevitable "if the trends in national indebtedness, low productivity increases, mediocre education performance and decaying social fabric are allowed to continue at the same time that massive American commitments of men, money and materials are made in different parts of the

14   globe." [2] Whatever the merit of the declinist view—and it does, indeed, have a certain irresistible logic to it—it is not basically affected by the successful prosecution of the gulf war. Indeed, insofar as the triumphant experience of the gulf war provides a boost for the advocates of military spending and new international commitments, it may be expected to perpetuate the very phenomenon of "imperial overstretch" against which Kennedy warns.

Finally, the gulf war shed little light on the prospects, or lack thereof, of a multipolar world. The crisis did demonstrate the continued resistance of Germany and Japan to the acceptance of political-military roles commensurate with their economic power. It does not follow, however, that multipolarity remains a pipedream, let alone that these states remain as dependent on American power today as they were yesterday. These conclusions once more reflect the assumption that force will remain as significant in the new world as it was in the old world.

★ ★ ★

That the gulf war was in large measure *sui generis* does not mean that it was insignificant. If the crisis did not reveal the future of international politics, it did point to the emergence of a certain disposition in American foreign policy that may indeed be highly significant. It is with the origins and nature of that disposition, and its dramatic manifestation in the gulf war, that this book is primarily concerned.

The United States is today the dominant military power in the world. In the reach and effectiveness of its military forces, America compares favorably with some of the greatest empires known to history. Rome reached barely beyond the compass of the Mediterranean, whereas Napoleon could not break out into the Atlantic and went to defeat in the vast Russian spaces. During the height of the so-called *Pax Britannica*, when the Royal Navy ruled the seas, Bismarck remarked that if the British army landed on the Prussian coast he would have it arrested by the local police. The United States has an altogether more formidable collection of forces than its predecessors among the world's great powers. It has global reach. It possesses the most technologically advanced arms, commanded by professionals skilled in the art of war. It can transport powerful continental armies over oceanic distances. Its historic adversaries are in retreat, broken by internal discord.

Under these circumstances, an age-old temptation—the imperial temptation—may prove compelling for the United States. That this temptation is pursued under the banner of a new world order, an order that promises to universalize both peace and the institutions of freedom, does not relieve its dangers. Nor are these dangers lessened by the consideration that the imperial temptation to which the nation succumbed in the gulf war—and to which it may yet fall victim again—involves not rule over others but the brief, massive use of military power in which the emphasis is placed on punishment and not rehabilitation. The nation is not likely to be attracted to the visions of empire that animated colonial powers of the past; it may well find attractive, however, a vision that enables the nation to assume an imperial role without fulfilling the classic duties of imperial rule.

The imperial temptation has arisen, in the first instance, because of the novel circumstances in international relations brought on by the end of the cold war. By virtue of the balance that existed in international politics during the cold war, which restrained both the Soviet Union and the United States, certain actions were foreclosed on both sides because they seemed altogether too dangerous. In the absence of a central balance, internal as opposed to external restraints on the use of force now have a greater importance than they formerly did. At the same time, however, these internal restraints have been weakened by the discovery of a way of war that enables the United States to throw the burdens of military conflict almost wholly onto the shoulders of the adversary. Moral and legal restraints on the use of force, which have always rested primarily on prudential considerations, have thus been considerably weakened. Under the right circumstances, this way of war enables us to go to war with greater precipitancy than we otherwise might while also allowing us to walk away from the ruin thus created without feeling a commensurate sense of responsibility.

Restraints, both internal and external, will doubtless continue to inhibit the use of American military power. How formi-

16   dable these barriers will be, however, is questionable. A public resentful of foreign aid and increasingly nationalistic may still give its approval to uses of American force that do not require inordinate outlays of blood and treasure. Traditional allies and former adversaries, who have their own reasons for maintaining good relations with the United States, may do the same. A nation resentful of its declining economic performance, which finds that its status as the world's only superpower rests above all on its military strength, may find itself tempted to demonstrate that its own peculiar asset, built up in the course of a rivalry that is no more, still has a continuing relevance in world politics. A president who believes—not without reason—that his popularity rests upon the conduct of foreign policy, and who found himself most in his element when exercising decisive leadership in war, may also face temptations of a similar kind. No historical inevitability decrees that the nation must make this fateful choice; on the contrary, its vital interests and its deepest purposes would best be served by a far different course. But the temptation exists.

It is the principal contention of this book that in the pursuit of a new world role, one required neither by security need nor by traditional conceptions of the nation's purpose, the Bush administration has given military force a position in our statecraft that is excessive and disproportionate. It has done so with the consent, and even enthusiasm, of the nation. That excess, and that disproportionality, are nowhere more apparent than in the readiness with which the United States went to war against Iraq, despite the availability of an alternative strategy that promised to secure American vital interests short of war. These traits are equally apparent in the readiness with which American leaders and the broader public are now prepared to consider measures of preventive war that the nation had previously deemed to be dangerous and wrong. They attest to the development in the United States of an attitude toward force that the nation embraces at its peril.

The peril is not preeminently to the nation's purse; it is to its soul. The danger is not so much that we will fail to protect our interests; it is that we will betray our historic ideals. By recalling those ideals in the course of this work, it is to be hoped that

Americans will realize that the nation has assumed traits it once shunned and adopted habits it once excoriated. There is no assumption made here that the nation has always lived up to its ideals; it did, however, always look up to them. We believe that it needs to do so again.

PART ONE

America's Road to the New World Order

CHAPTER 1

The Bush Administration
and the End
of Containment

The Bush administration came to office in 1989 with an outlook and commitment that emphasized the need for continuity over change in the nation's foreign policy. Despite the changes that had already occurred in Soviet internal politics and foreign policy, President Bush and his closest advisors gave no indication that they in any way anticipated that great events might be in train. Quite the contrary, the new administration began its tenure clearly skeptical of the optimism with which the outgoing president viewed future prospects for Soviet-American relations. Ronald Reagan had been the archetype of those who believed in the eternal and implacable hostility of the Soviet Union toward the West. Yet he had altered this belief by the time he left office in response to events occurring in the last two years of his presidency. Those same events apparently did not impress his successor to anywhere near the extent they had Mr. Reagan. Much less given than Reagan to ideological considerations, Bush was also less given to Reagan's leaps of imagination. The difference between the two was only partly a matter of temperament. It was also a reflection of the fact that, as president, Bush had a much greater stake in foreign policy than Reagan had. Although Reagan came to office at a critical moment in foreign policy, when the détente of the early 1970s had collapsed and a new cold war was taking shape, the nation's fortieth president regarded the reform of domestic policy to constitute his principal mandate. The Reagan Revolution, however incomplete and in many respects abortive, was in domestic not foreign policy. This is not to say that Reagan's impact

22   on foreign policy was negligible, only that foreign policy was never
seen as the raison d'être of his administration. Despite the considerable changes the Reagan years brought to American foreign
policy and to the nation's position in the world, the conduct of
external affairs remained for Reagan of secondary importance to
the conduct of domestic policy.

By contrast, it was apparent from the outset that for Bush
foreign policy was to be the principal activity and justification of
his administration. The American people, Richard Nixon once
remarked, do not need a president for domestic affairs, only for the
conduct of foreign policy. Bush evidently shared this view, just as
he shared Nixon's fascination with foreign policy. Coming to
office with the advantage of an impressive background in matters
of diplomacy and national security, Bush saw himself as having the
credentials of a professional. Whereas Reagan had been a rank
amateur in statecraft (though, as fate would have it, a very fortunate amateur), and had regarded external affairs as a largely
unwelcome intrusion, Bush was presumably an expert and, in the
manner of experts, lived to conduct foreign policy. This image
partly explains the difference between Reagan and Bush in the
conduct of foreign policy. Experts are not normally expected to
indulge grand visions; leaps of the imagination in statecraft are
seen as the telltale characteristic of amateurs. Indeed, to eschew
the visionary is considered an indispensable qualification of the
expert in a realm that is subject to the laws of necessity far more
than domestic politics. In relation to foreign policy, Bush's avowal
that he lacked the "vision thing" was more a reflection of the
expert's pride than an apology for not having the outlook of his
predecessor.

The end of the 1980s, however, was not the best of times for
the experts. The reign of the expert is in periods when the affairs of
states follow their accustomed course, not when events take a new
and quite unexpected turn. The sudden end of the cold war
overturned the political truths of the postwar world—truths by
which the experts had interpreted and understood this world. It
raised the issue that there might be still deeper forces at work in
the relations of nations, forces that might invalidate the political

truths believed to govern the postwar world. At the very least, the events of 1989 pointed to the need for looking anew at the world, a task for which the expert, even if willing to do so, might not be the best party.

The Bush administration came to office prepared to administer over the cold war. It had not assumed power in order to preside over a radical alteration of the nation's foreign policy, let alone a transformation of its role in the world. But the events of 1989 made it apparent that this position would not do. Slowly, the administration began to respond to changes that, by late fall, eventuated in the collapse of the Soviet Union's European empire. At year's end, a new and outwardly promising relationship had developed between the Soviet and American heads of state. By January 1990, after a year in office, an initially skeptical president appeared to have been converted into a true believer.

The conversion gave rise to problems, though, and not inconsiderable ones. So long as one remained a skeptic about the changes occurring in Soviet foreign policy, both a familiar American policy and role could be preserved, even if in altered form. But once skepticism had been abandoned, and the end of the cold war accepted, the task of redefining the nation's role and policy had to be confronted. The essential dimensions of that task were defined by a simple yet fundamental consideration: for the first time in over a half a century the United States was no longer confronted with a great power threat to its security. Such a threat had led the nation to abandon its policy of isolation and to intervene in World War II. A fascist victory would have endangered the nation's physical security and material well-being; it also held out the prospect of a world in which the institutions of freedom might perish, one in which the American example and influence would become irrelevant. A hostile world, from which America was shut out, would in turn affect the integrity of the nation's institutions and the quality of its domestic life. The threat to physical and economic security apart, it was to prevent this prospect from materializing that the United States abandoned its interwar isolationism and intervened in World War II.

24   The postwar policy of containment can be traced to roughly the same considerations. The domination of Western Europe by the Soviet Union would have threatened the nation's security. Containment responded in the first instance to the imperative of maintaining a balance of power and to the fear that Soviet control over Western Europe might shift the global balance decisively against the United States. At the same time, containment went beyond a conventional security interest and expressed a broader interest—coincident with the nation's purpose—in preserving and extending the institutions of freedom. Throughout the long postwar period, these two faces of containment, the organization of power and the vindication of purpose, had seldom been clearly distinguished by administrations despite the repeated efforts of critics to do so.

The events of 1989 put an end to containment. They did so by bringing to an end the division of Europe and of the postwar role of the Soviet Union in Europe. Mikhail Gorbachev was the symbol of this transformation, but its underlying cause was the rapidly deteriorating condition of the Soviet economy and the rampant social, political, and military disorganization the Soviet Union manifested. The end of Europe's division signaled the end of the threat that had prompted America's postwar policy, a threat that in its origins had been both military and ideological. In abandoning its European empire the Soviet Union abandoned not only its military but also what little remained of its ideological pretensions. The result was to leave the United States without a major military or ideological challenge. A long period in the nation's history had apparently come to an end. But if this was indeed the case, what then was the justification for persisting in the global role America had played since World War II? And if that role was no longer appropriate, given the recession of threats to the nation's security, what was America's new role to be?

These were large questions that sooner or later the Bush administration would have to address. In the brief period between the fall of the Berlin Wall and the outbreak of the crisis in the Persian Gulf, the administration began to grope for answers. Its initial reaction to the events of 1989 was simply to insist that the nation must continue to play a global role and to support a foreign policy commensurate with that role. This insistence sprang partially from the constraints imposed by a period of transition. But these constraints apart, the determination to maintain an essential continuity of role rested on the conviction that the post–cold war world would continue to need a power able to maintain peace and stability and that only the United States could fill this need. Even if the cold war had come to an end, the need for international order had not. Whether we welcomed it or not, the task of providing order to the world was the nation's inescapable lot, given its position as the world's greatest and most trusted power. To shoulder this task was not only a matter of duty but of vital interest as well, given the nation's stake in the effective functioning of the global economy and the spillover effects of instability elsewhere in the world on the nation's security.

The insistence that international stability required an essential continuity of role raised the question: what threatened stability? The answer that an American military withdrawal from Europe and Asia might do so was largely circular and raised the further question: why would an American withdrawal have this effect? Never explicitly articulated by the administration, the implicit answer was that in the absence of an American military presence the nations of Europe and Asia might once again return to their ancient ways. An American withdrawal presumably would create a power vacuum, which each country might fear being filled in a manner disadvantageous, and even threatening, to its security. Given this pervasive fear, the old game might well start up once again. It was to prevent this from occurring that the retention of existing arrangements was needed. The American military presence and the security arrangements that legitimized this presence remained indispensable for the reassurance a post–cold war world required to avoid instability.

In emphasizing the threat of instability at the center of the international system as the principal justification for preserving an essential continuity of role and policy, the administration followed a predictable course. It was in Europe that the great change in world politics had taken place, and it was to Europe that the

26   administration's response to the challenge of a new world was
above all directed. If that response seemed less than candid, it was
so largely because the principal source of future instability was seen
to be our major European ally, Germany (just as on the other side
of the world the principal source of instability was seen to be our
major Asian ally, Japan). America's continued presence in these
areas was needed primarily to reassure the neighbors of these
states, though how this might be done if the real source of anxiety
was their growing economic preponderance remained unclear. An
American military presence would not redress a growing economic
imbalance or the political influence that could be expected to
develop along with it. Against the expansion of German and
Japanese economic power, an American military presence appeared irrelevant. That same presence might forestall Germany
and Japan from seeking more independent military roles, particularly from acquiring nuclear weapons—a development that might
well lead to countermeasures by neighbors of these states. But
neither Germany nor Japan showed the slightest disposition to
embark on a course that had led in the past to war, defeat, and
grief. On the contrary, the evident advantages of their present
situation were such that there was little reason to think they would
abandon them. A collapse of the global economy might lead to
such abandonment. In all likelihood, however, it would also lead
to a withdrawal of the American military presence.

The Bush administration thus evoked fears of a return to the
old world as the justification for maintaining a role that had been
forged in response to the necessities arising from the cold war.
Still, it was undeniable that those necessities had changed and
that a new conception of role was required. The United States was
no longer the defender of freedom against the threat of Soviet
totalitarianism. If the endemic dangers of the old world nevertheless remained, it was necessary to acknowledge that the dangers
were not the same as those that had dominated the period of the
cold war. Being different in character, they required a different
vision of the nation's role. To maintain a peace that remained
fragile and subject to instability called more for a policeman than
the leader of a coalition confronted by a hostile and identifiable

adversary. In the new world the adversary was no longer identifia- ble in advance; the adversary was now instability and could mate- rialize in a variety of concrete guises.

If America's new role promised to be as dominant as its previous role had been—and this was clearly the vital element of the continuity held out by the administration—it also promised to be a much more complex and difficult role than that played in the long period of the cold war. From principal custodian of freedom against a specific adversary, America was now to become principal custodian of stability and order against any state threatening the tranquility of the international system. The difficulties inherent in the new dispensation were apparent. A nation that was accus- tomed to seeing itself as the exemplar and defender of freedom would find the role of policeman much less appealing and conse- quently could not be counted on to support its maintenance. This appeared to be the prospect even if the public accepted the need of the new role and equated that need with the nation's security interests. Neither of these conditions could be assumed.

Nor was it clear that the Bush administration would itself be content with a foreign policy whose principal function was that of providing the reassurance expected of a custodial role. In the months preceding the gulf crisis the administration often seemed less than persuaded by its own arguments on the need for main- taining continuity of role and policy. What it seemed sure of was the need, rather than the reasons for the need. This outlook ultimately stemmed from the simple conviction that the cold war had not been won only to relinquish America's global position. This conviction notwithstanding, the question persisted whether the role the administration had begun to articulate for the post– cold war world would be supported by the nation and accepted by our major allies. If the first half of 1990 afforded no clear answers, there were indications that the American policeman might hence- forth play an increasingly peripheral role in developments that were reshaping a region which had long formed the center of American interests and policy. Nothing seemed more revealing of this prospect than the July 1990 meeting in the Caucasus between the German and Soviet heads of state in which the final terms of

28   German unity were worked out. That the terms essentially corresponded with American policy was perhaps less significant than
the fact that they were arrived at without American participation
or prior approval. The Stavropol Agreement, even if it could not
reasonably be seen to raise the prospect of Soviet-German collu-
sion at the West's expense, pointed to a European future in which
the United States would no longer have anything approximating
the influence it had once enjoyed.

CHAPTER 2

The New World Order

There is an apparent simplicity to most of the major statements on American foreign policy that readily lends them to caricature. Bush's vision of a "new world order" is no exception to what has now become a virtual tradition. Initially set forth at the outset of the gulf crisis in a presidential address to Congress, the new world order was depicted as one "where the rule of law supplants the rule of the jungle . . . in which nations recognize the shared responsibility for freedom and justice . . . where the strong respect the rights of the weak." This was the prospective world made possible by the end of the cold war; it was the prospective world that Saddam Hussein placed in jeopardy by his act of naked aggression against Kuwait. If this new world "struggling to be born" was to have a chance of surviving, the president insisted, the test posed by Iraq must be met. In the circumstances, President Bush declared, America had no alternative but to "support the rule of law" and to "stand up to aggression." "Had we not responded to this first provocation with clarity of purpose; if we do not continue to demonstrate our determination; it would be a signal to actual and potential despots around the world." Failure to respond to the Iraqi aggression would thus deal a fatal blow to a hopeful future, just as resisting the aggressor would set a precedent in building a peaceful and just international order.[1]

This first and perhaps most striking statement on the new world order was made at a time when there were few intimations that the American government would eventually employ force to secure the liberation of Kuwait. Four months later, the United

30   States went to war against Iraq. In his State of the Union message, given two weeks after the outbreak of the conflict, the president again took up the theme that he evidently considered central to an understanding of the gulf crisis. "What is at stake," Mr. Bush declared, "is more than one small country, it is a big idea—a new world order where diverse nations are drawn together in common cause to achieve the universal aspirations of mankind: peace and security, freedom and the rule of law. Such is a world worthy of our struggle. . . . " The new world order "where brutality will go unrewarded, and aggression will meet collective resistance," could be achieved, however, only if the United States accepted the burden of leadership that was indispensable to its realization. At this "defining hour" in the nation's history, the president concluded, America was "the only nation on this earth that could assemble the forces of peace."[2]

On the morrow of victory over Iraq, the president, in addressing a joint session of Congress, returned to the same themes. A new world order, he averred, was now "a very real prospect." The United Nations, "freed from cold war stalemate, is poised to fulfill the historic vision of its founders." This did not mean, he noted in an allusion to a war that made up a now distant past, that victory over Iraq was waged as "a war to end all wars." The new world order "cannot guarantee an era of perpetual peace. But enduring peace must be our mission."[3]

Although the advent of the new world order was fortuitous, the vision and role it proclaimed were not. The gulf crisis provided the unanticipated occasion to articulate a role the Bush administration had been steadily moving toward, however indirectly and perhaps only half-consciously. The significance of the crisis was not that it suddenly illuminated interests in the Persian Gulf of which the American government had been previously unaware. The strategic importance of the gulf, owing to the concentration of energy resources there, had long been recognized by American administrations, as was the vital interest of the United States in protecting Saudi Arabia from being taken over by a power that might use the Saudis' enormous oil reserves for purposes inimical to Western interests. By 1990 these considerations passed for conventional wisdom in American foreign policy. What was significant about the onset and course of the crisis was the fact that the American response to Iraq's invasion of Kuwait was ultimately justified in terms of a vision of world order and of the leading role America would play in the achievement of that order. A grand design that prior to the crisis had remained unarticulated and partially obscured even to its architects was now laid bare.

In considering the origins of the new world order, it is useful to recall the historic pronouncement that marked the great transformation in post–World War II American foreign policy. The Truman Doctrine was immediately occasioned by a crisis in the eastern Mediterranean that was precipitated by Great Britain's inability to continue in the dominant role it had long played in the region. The fear of a communist victory in the Greek civil war as well as the fear that Turkey might prove unable to stand up to increasing Soviet pressure led President Truman to request of Congress on March 12, 1947, that aid be given these two states. The expansion of Soviet influence in the eastern Mediterranean was seen as endangering not only the still precarious security position of a war-devastated Western Europe but Western interests in the Middle East as well.

While the Truman Doctrine responded to a specific threat, it did so within the framework of a sweeping vision of world order and of an equally sweeping view of the American commitment to, and role in, securing that order. The vision was nothing less than a world free from aggression, a world in which free peoples might work out their own destinies in their own way, a world that made possible the lasting freedom and independence of all nations. The commitment and role were nothing less than protagonist and champion in securing this world. "I believe," President Truman declared to Congress and the nation, "that it must be the policy of the United States to support free peoples who are resisting attempted subjugation by armed minorities or by outside pressures. I believe that we must assist free peoples to work out their own destinies in their own way."[4] Containment formed the eventual policy expression of the vision of world order and the conception of role held out in the Truman Doctrine.

32   The Truman Doctrine was a historic pronouncement because of what it foreshadowed. Will the same be said one day of Bush's new world order? Will the statements of the president in the Persian Gulf crisis be seen in retrospect to delineate the essential rationale of American foreign policy for the post–cold war period, much as the Truman Doctrine did for the period of the cold war? Whatever answer history may ultimately give to these questions they cannot simply be dismissed by the response that the new world order consisted of little more than vaporous generalities whose meaning probably remained obscure even to its author. It is useful to recall that much the same criticism was once made of the Truman Doctrine. At the time, a number of critics insisted that the Truman Doctrine, with its apparently unlimited commitment to help "free peoples to work out their destinies in their own way," its sense of universal crisis which required every nation to choose "between alternative ways of life," and its messianic hope of redeeming history by making possible the "lasting freedom and independence for all nations," was a perfect expression of the American penchant for thinking about foreign policy in great abstractions, or, to use an expression of the time, in "globalist" terms–that is, in terms which had little tangible relation to the specific circumstances attending and limiting foreign policy.

What was once said of the Truman Doctrine is said again today of the new world order. The criticism may prove as irrelevant in grasping the broader significance of this most recent presidential vision as it was in grasping the broader significance of the earlier vision. The eventual policy implications of the new world order are neither more nor less apparent than were the eventual policy implications of the Truman Doctrine. The criticism, in effect, that visions lack policy specifics, that their operational meaning is unclear, is as true as it is irrelevant. The common and essential characteristic of the grand foreign policy pronouncements of presidents is a general disposition—a certain orientation—that is broadly indicative of a direction in foreign policy, yet neither indicates, let alone determines, the specifics of policy. This is only to say that the fate of a vision is left largely to the mercy of events (both at home and abroad). Had there been no Korean War, the policy of containment might well have developed quite differently. At the same time, the fact that the Korean War led to the consequences it did cannot be properly understood without seeing those consequences in terms of the vision—the general disposition—that made them possible.

These considerations should serve to caution against a ready dismissal of the new world order. Having had a war in its name, there is reason enough to take seriously the vision it expresses. There is all the more reason to do so when the events antecedent to that war are recalled. For the gulf crisis was preceded, as we have noted, by a period in which the future of American foreign policy and of the American role in the world were the objects of extensive reconsideration. The new world order did not simply emerge out of the blue, the product of a passing need to find an appealing justification for the course the administration had determined to take in the Persian Gulf. The term itself may have been the product of happenstance, as was widely reported at the time. But the disposition it expressed was no more the product of happenstance than the disposition expressed in the Truman Doctrine. The crisis that arose in 1947 in the eastern Mediterranean could not have elicited a declaration of the character it did had it not been for the larger issues at stake which had preoccupied the Truman administration for some time. The decision to give aid to Greece and Turkey helped to crystallize these larger issues by placing them in a broader framework. In much the same way, the Bush administration's decision to intervene in the gulf served to crystallize and place in a broader context the larger issues of role that had preoccupied the administration in the immediate wake of the cold war.

★　★　★

There is little difficulty in setting out the principal elements that make up the new world order. Undoubtedly the most important was the end of the cold war. The collapse of Soviet power made possible the vision of the Bush administration. That vision did not

34   respond to the time-honored compulsions of the balance of power, for with the virtual disappearance of Soviet power and influence there was no longer a hostile great power against which American power had to provide the balance. This was the simple meaning of the claim, endlessly repeated, that the United States had emerged as the sole superpower in the world, or, as some would put it, the sole imperial power. A rare moment in history had presumably been reached, one that opened the prospect of a world order that could not be aspired to in an international system governed by the age-old requirements of the balance of power.

A policy that need no longer respond to balance of power requirements is one that, almost by definition, is no longer concerned with a great power threat. The Truman Doctrine, and the policy of containment to which it led, responded to what was seen as a Soviet threat to the balance—a threat that was centered in Europe. The initial critical measures of containment, the Marshall Plan and the North Atlantic Alliance, expressed the vital American interest in preserving the security and independence of the nations of Western Europe. In the context of Soviet-American rivalry, they constituted a clear acknowledgment that the domination of Western Europe by the Soviet Union might shift the global balance decisively against the United States, thereby giving rise to a security problem which would severely strain the nation's resources and, in time, even jeopardize its democratic institutions.

The Truman Doctrine and containment responded not only to what was seen as a military threat but also to what was seen as a formidable political-ideological threat. Indeed, to many it was the latter threat that was judged to be much more significant. In the Soviet claim to represent a new form of political and social organization having universal significance, the militant standard-bearer of communism in the postwar world was considered to pose an unprecedented challenge to America's historic role and purpose. Given this challenge and the nation's sensitivity to it, from the outset of the cold war American security was interpreted as a function of both a balance of power between states and the inter-

nal order maintained by states. The balance that formed the **35**
dominant objective of American postwar policy was both military
and ideological.

By contrast, the new world order was not a response to an
imperiled global balance. Bush's vision of a new world order
responded to the threat posed by middle or small powers, that is,
by states which did not and could not threaten the balance. These
states, moreover, appeared without exception to come from the
ranks of the developing world. Despite their size, the threat they
were seen to pose to other states—particularly the developed
states—was considerable. This was so for a number of reasons but
above all because weapons of mass destruction, along with their
means of delivery, threatened to become increasingly available
even to states of only modest means. The expectation was that in
terms of sheer aggressiveness and resentment of these lesser powers
toward those who dominate the international system, there would
be future Iraqs. These future Iraqs need not enjoy a financial base
comparable to that of Iraq in order to prove dangerous. All they
need is the ability to obtain a small stockpile of weapons of mass
destruction and the willingness to use them.

The principal threat, then, to which the new world order
responded was a threat posed by middle to small developing powers
on the periphery of the international system. The importance of
this threat was not in its relationship to the center, as was the case
during the cold war. It was not because any threat arising on the
periphery might affect the center, and thus the global balance,
that gave it significance. It was of course possible that even in the
new world great power relations might be adversely affected by
conflicts on the periphery, but this prospect did not form the
principal justification for the administration's design. The justification was to be found in the periphery itself. The prospect of
future Iraqs—lawless, renegade states in possession of modern
weapons, including those capable of mass destruction, and
dedicated to the pursuit of aggressive, even terrorist, ends—was
the danger. If allowed to go unchecked, these states, by virtue of
their threat to international order, might well come to represent

36   the functional equivalent today of the great power threat of yesterday. *

According to the Bush administration, this prospective development holds out the most serious threat to American security in the period ahead. The great object of a policy of intervention is thus one of keeping weapons of mass destruction from falling into the hands of aggressive and expansionist states. In the wake of the gulf crisis, it is above all the prevention of nuclear proliferation that provides the justification for an interventionist policy. Although this policy would presumably be directed only against aggressive governments, it may prove quite difficult to determine those states that cannot be trusted with the possession of nuclear weapons. Until Iraq invaded Kuwait, it is useful to recall, the American government apparently had yet to determine that Baghdad could not be entrusted with nuclear weapons. Given this experience, administration policymakers may be expected to act on the side of caution and to impose quite strict tests for determin-

---

* A defense strategy, corresponding to the political dictates of the new world order, would focus the nation's efforts on "regional contingencies"—that is, principally on regional conflicts in the developing world—and on maintaining the forward military presence needed to deter such conflicts. In the course of the gulf war, the Secretary of Defense articulated the new strategy for America's defense. The war against Iraq, Dick Cheney declared, "presages very much the type of conflict we are most likely to confront again in this new era—major regional contingencies against foes well armed with advanced conventional and unconventional weaponry. In addition to southwest Asia, we have important interests in Europe, Asia, the Pacific, and Central and Latin America. In each of these regions there are opportunities and potential future threats to our interests. We must configure our policies and our forces to effectively deter, or quickly defeat, such future regional threats." Iraq not only illustrated the potential of regional instability threatening to America's interests, the secretary went on to point out, but also the growing problem of the proliferation of weapons of mass destruction. "By the year 2000, it is estimated that at least 15 developing nations will have the ability to build ballistic missiles—eight of which either have or are near to acquiring nuclear capabilities. Thirty countries will have chemical weapons, and ten will be able to deploy biological weapons as well." (Statement of Secretary of Defense Dick Cheney in connection with the FY 1992–93 Department of Defense Budget, Senate Armed Services Committee, February 21, 1991, p. 7, mimeo.)

ing those states that can be regarded as trustworthy. If so, a wider net may have to be fashioned than one designed to catch only the Iraqs and the North Koreas. Yet the wider the net, the more burdensome the policy may be to implement.

The new world order thus appeared to reverse the postwar geopolitical priorities of American foreign policy. The security threat it identified as critical for the 1990s had previously drawn its significance largely from its relation to a conflict that in 1990 had all but disappeared. Yet it was not only the East-West conflict that in the past gave significance to the south. In the 1970s, the developing world was not only considered important in its own right; at that time the relationships between the developed and developing states were deemed by many to have displaced the cold war in significance. It was the developing world that presumably held out the more serious and the ever growing threat to the developed states of the West. It did so, the prevailing view held, not only because of its possession of natural resources indispens-able to the industrialized states but because of its power—the power of the weak—to transmit misery in the form of chaos and war.

In part, that power took a passive form and was a function of the cold war. The poor and developing states were seen as a dangerous magnet for superpower rivalry. The power to transmit misery would, it was argued, eventually take an active form. Scenarios were evoked of a world in which governments of poor states, at once increasingly revolutionary in outlook yet unable to raise the living standards of their ever burgeoning populations, would threaten desperate measures against the rich nations to compel them to undertake a massive transfer of wealth to the world's poor. An otherwise fanciful future was given plausibility by the assumption that nuclear weapons would become increasingly available, even to states with modest resources, and that the possession of only a small number of these weapons might effec-tively be used to coerce the rich into making concessions to the poor that otherwise would not have been made.

In the 1970s, the challenge of the developing world—the periphery of American foreign policy—was seen primarily as a

38   challenge to great and growing inequalities of wealth. Unless these inequalities were reduced, the prevailing argument ran, a serious threat to international order and stability was inevitable. In what appeared to be a reversal of the "natural" order of things, the poor and weak states of the world were found to pose grave peril to the rich and strong. They were found to do so in part because it was assumed that rising moral and material costs of employing force would increasingly inhibit the strong from resorting to force against the weak. To this was added the belief that in an interdependent world the strong (and rich) could not separate their fate from the weak (and poor). Moral considerations apart, it was the world's interdependence—an interdependence of which nuclear weapons provided the most striking manifestation—that compelled the developed states out of self-interest to reduce the disparities of wealth in the world.

The prevailing response then to the challenge supposedly being mounted by the developing world was to search for ways to accommodate the challenge. If a number of states on the periphery threatened to behave in an aggressive manner, the threat was a compelling reason for making a special effort to come to terms with them. The favored strategy for dealing with the rebellious nations in the developing world was to seek to appease them without paying an exorbitant price. That strategy fell into disfavor in the 1980s. A revived cold war and the realization that the case of oil was unique served to diminish markedly the significance that had been given to the challenge of the developing world. As the significance attached to the challenge to international order and stability diminished, so did the disposition to respond to its manifestations by searching for terms of accommodation.

In its emphasis on the importance of threats to international order arising on the periphery, the Bush new world order harkened back to the concerns of the 1970s. Its understanding of these threats and of the means for dealing with them, however, bore little relation to the outlook of a generation before. Whereas then errant and aggressive behavior was attributed largely to a deep sense of frustration with, and resentment toward, a world marked by radical inequalities of wealth and power, the Bush administra-

tion considered such behavior to be without much deeper signifi-   **39**
cance than the behavior itself. Previously, aggressive behavior,
particularly when directed toward the West, was commonly seen
as rooted in the wrongs of a colonial past, but Bush considered
such behavior independently of a history that might be used in
some measure to justify it.

If these changes over a generation in outlook and understanding reflected in the new world order were partially obscured during
the gulf crisis, it was because Iraq's invasion of Kuwait was seen on
almost all sides as a case of "pure aggression"—an instance of
aggression that was without so much as a shadow of justification.
Even so, the significance of the new world order transcended the
circumstances marking the crisis that occasioned its appearance.
The several presidential and other authoritative articulations of
this vision suggested that its architects had abjured the search for
reasons that might account for aggressive behavior just as they had
abandoned efforts to address the conditions that might have bred
such behavior.

In its understanding of the causes and means of treatment of
aggression, the new world order built on an analogy to the causes
and consequences of unlawful violence in domestic society. It did
so by relying on a particular view of the proper and effective means
for the prevention of aggressive behavior, one that stressed a
reliance upon punishment rather than rehabilitation. According
to this view, even if it were acknowledged that there might be
deep-seated causes for aggressive behavior, attempts to respond to
those causes would only serve to exacerbate the problem. History
showed the importance of stopping aggressors at the outset, for the
pathology of aggression is such that it never expires of its own
accord. This explains why it is necessary not to negotiate with
aggressors, let alone to appease or reward them in any way—a
treatment that would only serve to encourage them. In President
Bush's formula for dealing with Iraq—"no negotiations, no compromises, no attempts at face-saving and no rewards for aggression"—the outlook informing the new world order was given
succinct, yet complete, expression.[5]

40   The need to stand up to aggressors—by denying, containing, disarming, or, if necessary, destroying them—imposed a considerable burden on the United States as the nation which, in the president's words, "must bear a major share of leadership in this effort." It was an inescapable burden, though, for it was only America that had "both the moral standing and the means to . . . assemble the forces of peace." [6] The world must have order and order presupposes, even necessitates, a guarantor. Not surprisingly, the theme of the responsibilities of power suffused Bush's vision of the new world order. Yet these responsibilities were not undertaken only for others but for ourselves as well. The new world order was justified quite as much in terms of America's security as it was in terms of the security of other nations. The fusion of interested and disinterested elements which together comprised the rationale of the new world order, the insistence that what we intend to do for others we are also doing for ourselves, and what we fail to do for others we also fail to do for ourselves, were thoroughly familiar. The same themes found prominent expression in the Truman Doctrine. A willingness "to help free people to maintain their free institutions and their national integrity against aggressive movements," President Truman declared, "is no more than a frank recognition that totalitarian regimes imposed on free people, by direct or indirect aggression, undermine the foundations of international peace and hence the security of the United States." This was the essential rationale for the policy of containment, as it was for the subsequent interventions—notably Korea and Vietnam—undertaken in pursuit of containment. The new world order thus followed a well-marked path.

In its universalism—its commitment to protect the political independence and territorial integrity of all states—the new world order was again reminiscent of the Truman Doctrine. It differed from the great post–World War II pronouncement, however, in its undertaking to work through the United Nations (UN). The Truman Doctrine did not quite signal the abandonment of American efforts to work through the UN, but it was a clear indication that the United States was ready to pursue its major foreign policy objectives by other means if necessary, including unilateral means. By contrast, Bush's pronouncements during the gulf crisis promised to give the UN a position it had not had in American foreign policy even at the end of World War II.

The commitment to the UN expressed in the new world order appeared to bring to an end the long period, coincident with the cold war, during which the organization played a negligible role in the nation's foreign policy. It was argued that the prominent role now given to the UN was not unalterable, that its future role would depend upon its effectiveness in dealing with "threats to the peace, breaches of the peace, and acts of aggression," and that in making a determination in this matter the American government would apply its own criteria of effectiveness. The conclusion drawn from these considerations was that if the UN failed to fulfill American expectations, as it once failed to do, this nation would again turn to other institutional means for pursuing its purposes. Given the solitude of the United States as a military power and the absence of the former need to enlist the power of others, a return to unilateralism in foreign policy represented an increasingly attractive prospect. In the wake of the war against Iraq, President Bush indicated as much in noting that if the UN Security Council had not responded effectively to Iraq's aggression against Kuwait, the American government would have acted on its own.

On this view, what was important in the vision of world order entertained by the Bush administration was the leadership role America would play, not the institutional means of exercising this role. Yet the manner by which the nation's leadership would be exercised in the future was not simply a question of convenience. In Bush's vision, the UN was not a mere adornment of a new world order made in America, an adornment that might be cast off at will once the constraints it imposed on action became unduly irritating, let alone truly burdensome. Undoubtedly, the constraints might always be thrown off, but the relevant issue was how great a price would be paid for doing so. Even those who resisted tying American foreign policy to the UN, as the architects of the new world order did, nevertheless conceded that the tie might well be important for maintaining domestic support for an interven-

42   tionist policy. This did not show that the public would refuse support to unilateral action, regardless of circumstance. It did show, however, that a substantially greater measure of support would be given to action that bore a multilateral character, particularly in circumstances in which a compelling security interest was not apparent.

CHAPTER 3

Aggression and Collective Security

The new world order joined a distinctive conception of the nature of international order with the idea of America's leadership. Neither element was novel. The analogy drawn between the problems of domestic and international order has been a recurrent theme of American diplomacy in this century. Equally persistent has been the conviction that international order implies this nation's leadership. The two elements are not casually related; they are not considered the accidental product of transient circumstance. They are seen, for all practical purposes, as inseparable. The essential condition for America's participation in the task of constructing a satisfactory international order has been our leadership in that task. This leadership imposes special responsibilities others do not have, but it also confers a degree of freedom others do not enjoy. In this manner, our acceptance of multilateralism has been conditioned by our ability, bordering on a right, to act unilaterally. Bush's vision of a new world order expressed what is by now a traditional outlook.

The assumption that the task of preventing aggression and securing peace in international society forms a close parallel to the same problem in domestic society is deeply embedded in the American consciousness. In either case, the forces of aggression constitute no more than a small minority when compared with the community of peace-loving people. In both cases, the circumstances from which aggression springs are essentially the same. Aggression occurs because aggressors miscalculate the determination and strength of those who will ultimately be ranged against

44   them. They are tempted to miscalculate because peace-loving peoples frequently fail to make clear their determination to resist aggression and to impress potential aggressors with the consequences they must expect should they once take the path of violence.

This failure was all too apparent in the case of Iraq, as the Bush administration reluctantly acknowledged. Iraq's miscalculation recalled the circumstances that 40 years earlier attended the outbreak of the Korean War. That war was also seen as resulting from the miscalculation of the aggressor, a miscalculation encouraged by the failure of an administration to make clear the consequences of aggression. It also recalled what John Foster Dulles termed the "profound lesson" of Korea: "Peace requires anticipating what it is that tempts an aggressor and letting him know in advance that, if he does not exercise self-control, he may face a hard fight, a losing fight. The Korean War . . . should finally have taught us that, if we can foresee aggression which will cause us to fight, we should let this be known, so that the potential aggressor will take this into calculation."[1] The Truman administration failed to heed this lesson, just as the Bush administration failed to heed it.

The conviction that aggression occurs because aggressors miscalculate implies that aggression is not only an evil but an unnecessary evil. States need not, in this view, resort to force to secure justice or to ensure their security; there are no conflicts of interest so intractable that force is the only solution. When states resort to force they choose a course they might have avoided and, accordingly, should have avoided. For this reason alone, the aggressive use of force—the deliberate choice of war as an instrument of national policy—may never be justified. Nor may it be justified if the world is ever to realize the prospect of an enduring peace. Both order and justice require that states not resort to force save as a measure of self or collective defense against an armed attack, or in accordance with the will of the international community as embodied in the decisions of the competent bodies of the UN.

In international as in domestic society, then, the proscription of force is not to be qualified by the nature of the causes that might have prompted its initiation. Whatever these causes, they **45** are not considered to justify the initiation of force; whatever a state's grievances, they do not sanction aggression. In setting forth the American position on the prosecution of German leaders for having committed crimes against peace, the American prosecutor declared before the International Military Tribunal at Nuremberg: "Our position is that whatever grievances a nation may have, however objectionable it finds that *status quo*, aggressive warfare is an illegal means for settling those grievances or for altering those conditions." [2] This near absolute condemnation of aggressive war goes back to Woodrow Wilson and has been subscribed to by administrations ever since. It was a central principle of a proposed agreement with Japan put forth by the United States in its last note to that country prior to the outbreak of war in the Pacific; it was the gravamen of the American indictment of the action taken by Great Britain and France against Egypt in 1956; and it was held to be the central principle at stake in Vietnam, as the Johnson administration never tired of insisting. The same principle was invoked by the American government in setting out on a course of action that led ultimately to war with Iraq, and President Bush has made it the centerpiece of his vision of world order.

Although the new world order made the proscription of the aggressive use of force its first and foremost principle, it did not simply equate peace with justice. As in the past, this latest expression of the American concept of international order did not acknowledge peace to be a higher value than justice. Peace and justice were still considered as two sides of the same coin. The order Bush sought was an order based on justice. Even so, the emphasis on order was clearly more pronounced than in the past, as was the conviction that states or, for that matter, peoples aspiring to statehood, need not resort to force to obtain justice. The case of Iraq gave considerable support to this emphasis on order. The gulf war provided a textbook example in support of the view that aggression is not only an evil but an unnecessary evil.

Taken at face value, the conviction that force need never be employed aggressively implies that the dilemma of choosing between peace and the preservation of other interests should never

46   arise. Experience, including our own, shows that it does arise. It did so most recently in the course of implementing the policy of containment. When this dilemma did arise, it was in part resolved by interpreting the prohibition on force so as to fit the requirements of containment, a task that was facilitated by the view that what constitutes aggression is not self-evident. Throughout the period of the cold war, care was taken that the prohibition on force was not interpreted to preclude the application of aggression to situations in which civil conflicts were supported in varying degrees by outside powers. Successive administrations were committed to the position that "indirect aggression" might be assimilated, and certainly in its more aggravated form could be assimilated, to an armed attack, thus justifying measures of self or collective defense. At the outset of the great contest, the Truman Doctrine spoke of "direct or indirect" aggression, just as it committed the United States to the support of free peoples resisting subjugation by armed minorities and by outside pressures. In the last years of the cold war, the Reagan Doctrine resolved the ambiguity attending the concept of aggression by casting aside the constraints it imposed and openly asserting the right to intervene in support of rebel movements struggling to overthrow communist governments.

The necessities of the cold war, real or alleged, thus not only led to the expansion of the concept of aggression well beyond its core meaning but even to its partial abandonment. In the region of America's historic sphere of influence, the Caribbean and Central America, it cannot be said to have ever been taken very seriously, as the several interventions from the 1950s through the 1980s attest. The nation's claim to a right to intervene there, when in its judgment interest so required, continued to be asserted after cold war necessities could no longer plausibly be invoked. Less than a year before proclaiming the new world order, President Bush intervened militarily in Panama, though his stated reasons for doing so—the protection of the Panama Canal and of American nationals in that country—were generally seen as little more than a *pro forma* justification for removing a dictator who had defied Washington once too often. Acting unilaterally and for reasons that would not have been sanctioned either by the UN or by the Organization of American States, Operation Just Cause scarcely seemed to form an appropriate prelude to the new world order.

This record of departure from the first and foremost principle of world order, together with the lesson it conveys, no longer appeared relevant for the Bush administration. With the end of the cold war the compulsions that once operated on policy did so no longer. What past departures on the whole demonstrated was the difficulty that could arise in reconciling the proscription of force with the preservation of interests deemed vital. The principal source of that difficulty was apparent: the proscription of force, if taken seriously, presupposed an international political reality that did not exist. American containment policy, however, responded to a political reality—the balance of power—that required the occasional departure from principle if interests other than peace were to be preserved. The governing requirement of containment was that a hostile Soviet Union not be allowed to expand its power and influence in areas of vital interest. Containment did not and could not create and maintain an order by the methods and restraints of the UN Charter, but by the traditional methods of countering hostile and expansionist power with power. The Cuban missile crisis was only the most dramatic illustration that these methods could not always be reconciled with the principle forbidding the initial use of force.

Nor was it only the familiar necessities of the balance of power that made a disparity between principle and practice inevitable. In America's case, the necessities of maintaining a favorable "internal" balance, by extending the institutions of freedom, did so as well. The optimistic assumption that the proscription of aggression would always result in such extension was never subscribed to in practice without qualification. Even in doctrine, it was never given unguarded endorsement. As already noted, the Truman Doctrine did not do so. Instead, it equivocated between the commitment to the cause of freedom and the commitment to abstain from forcible intervention in the internal affairs of states. Where the Truman Doctrine equivocated, the Reagan Doctrine

48   simply abandoned any pretense of reconciling an interest in order with an interest in universal freedom.

For the Bush administration, these dilemmas of force were no longer apparent. In the new world order the necessities imposed by the balance of power were assumed to be no longer operative, for there was no longer a great power against which American military power had to be balanced. Nor were the necessities incurred in maintaining a favorable internal balance operative in the sense they once were. While the extension of the institutions of freedom might remain a relevant policy for the nation, the motives for such a policy would no longer arise from a threat to these institutions.

By virtue of the great changes that had transformed the world, the proscription of aggression was no longer seen to raise the problems it once did. Because of these changes, a conception of international order previously subscribed to only as an ideal was endowed by Bush with practical relevance. In this conception, the condemnation and repression of aggression cannot be qualified by the identity of the aggressor. Aggression is aggression, whether it is committed by a small or a great power. Any attempt to distinguish between aggressive states on the basis of their power rather than on the basis of their actions would presumably be as inimical to international order as the attempt to make the same distinction between individual aggressors would be for civil society. In its response to Iraq's aggression against Kuwait there was no acknowledgment, tacit or otherwise, by the American government that the course of action taken toward Iraq was conditioned by considerations of relative power. The refusal to negotiate with the aggressor, let alone to consider any compromise with him, was supposedly dictated by the same considerations that rule out negotiating or compromising with those resorting to violence in domestic society. To reward aggression in any way is simply to encourage it. Not only must aggressors go unrewarded but they must be punished as well, else there would be little incentive to potential aggressors to refrain from following in their footsteps.

In resorting to aggression, the aggressor state has forfeited its rights. This being so, the means for achieving political objectives that are condemned prior to the initiation of force by an aggressor may become the means by which those objectives are realized by those who undertake a war of self or collective defense against aggression. In the Korean War, the initial objective of U.S. and UN forces was simply to push the invading forces of North Korea back to the thirty-eighth parallel, the boundary that had separated North and South Korea—in President Truman's words, "to restore peace there and to restore the border."[3] Within a very brief period, though, this objective changed to that of uniting Korea, an objective that could be achieved only by the invasion of North Korea and the complete defeat of North Korean forces. Still later, and subsequent to China's intervention in the conflict, the objective reverted back to the restoration of the border at the thirty-eighth parallel. Yet, throughout, American purposes were defined as simply "to resist aggression and to restore peace."[4]

Korea affords an instructive example of the willingness to use force—once force is defensively employed against aggression—to attain political objectives that, prior to the resort to force, were to be sought only by peaceful means. Thus the same means for achieving political objectives that are condemned in the case of the aggressor may become the means by which these very objectives are realized by those who undertake a war of self or collective defense. A necessary relationship is assumed to exist between the circumstances in which force is initiated and the objectives for which force is employed. Whereas the purposes of the aggressor state are by definition unjust, the purposes of those waging a defensive war against aggression must be just, again by definition.

A war fought not only to prevent an aggressor from achieving his immediate aims but to prevent future aggressions, whether by this aggressor or by other would-be aggressors, best fulfills the purposes of a defensive war. It does so despite the possibility that its consequences may go far beyond those traditionally associated with the conditions of a defensive war. It is not the restoration of the status quo that those resisting aggression wish to achieve but an outcome that promises to prevent the recurrence of aggression. This outcome was promised on more than one occasion by President Bush in the course of the gulf crisis. It afforded the principal justification for a military strategy that sought the destruction not

50   only of Iraq's military power in being but of its industrial infrastructure as well.

In recent decades, a sustained and effective criticism has been made of the several assumptions that form the basis for the concept of international order on which the Bush administration's vision rested. These assumptions, for the most part, coincide with the assumptions that comprise the idea of collective security. Accordingly, the now familiar criticism of collective security is also applicable to the vision of a new world order and may be summarized in this manner: whereas the essence of a traditional statecraft is discrimination on the basis of power, interest, and circumstance, the essence of collective security, and of the new world order, is precisely the absence of discrimination on the basis of these same factors. To the former, it makes all the difference whether aggression is committed by a small or a great power. To the latter, this distinction is irrelevant. To the former, a state's geographic position must normally determine its response to aggression. To the latter, geographic position as well must be viewed as irrelevant. Aggression is aggression, irrespective of the identity of the aggressor; the indivisibility of peace precludes a response determined by considerations of geography.

The refusal in principle to discriminate among aggressions on grounds of power, interest, and circumstance of course reflects the domestic analogy on which the idea of collective security rests. An international society is assumed, a society that bears a meaningful resemblance to domestic society. The state-members of this greater society have rights and duties much as the individuals that form domestic society have rights and duties. In both, the principal right of the members is that of security against physical attack, and the principal duty is that of abstaining from the initiation of armed force. In both, the members are held collectively responsible for maintaining the peace of the community to which they belong (though how this responsibility is carried out must depend upon the degree of organization of the community). In either, the attempt to distinguish acts of aggression on the basis of the circumstances attending each act must prove ruinous to the peace of the community, for such attempts must risk giving to the strong what is denied to the weak.

The great difficulty with this conception of international order is that it rests on a misunderstanding of the nature of the peace that exists within domestic society. Domestic peace is not threatened in the first instance by the errant behavior of individuals but by the deep dissatisfaction of large groups. It is not maintained by the impartial application of objective criteria to individuals but by reconciling the aims and aspirations of groups, a process that cannot be undertaken on the basis of the impartial application of objective criteria. It is by the processes of politics rather than of law that the peace of domestic society is maintained.

The rigid legalism that informs the idea of collective security is at odds with the outlook that characterizes the political process. It sees the attempt to understand the motives that led to aggression as an attempt to condone aggression. The historical context in which an act of aggression has arisen is swept aside for a formal interpretation of events that discourages the compromises which are the lifeblood of politics. In the name of peace and justice, the crime that has been committed against the international community must be punished, else potential aggressors will be encouraged to carry out their designs. To the end of punishment, states are expected to subordinate their particular interests which are, in any event, considered morally inferior to the collective interests of the international community. The necessity or the desirability of all states participating, as a matter of principle, in a war against a disturber of the peace is unquestioned. If peace is indivisible, as collective security contends, war in response to aggression must be universal.

These considerations notwithstanding, a conception of international order that the experience of this century has dealt harshly with was revived in the course of the gulf crisis, though in an entirely unexpected manner. It was revived not because a true community of power suddenly materialized where none existed before but because a hegemonial power emerged where before there had been a balance of power. The new world order pro-

52   claimed by the Bush administration was not an order of collective security in the sense that the champions of that system had always imagined. Still, if it was to develop and persist, it would be an order that might achieve the purposes that collective security was designed to achieve. It would do so, however, not because a "new and more wholesome" diplomacy founded upon general principles of law and justice had at last triumphed over the old diplomacy, as Woodrow Wilson once prophesied it would, but because American power had become unchallenged.

CHAPTER 4

Visions of Order:
Past and Present

I t is striking that at the outset of the 1990s Americans found themselves debating the desirability of a role that only a few years before would have been scornfully dismissed by those charged with the conduct of the nation's foreign policy. For the authors of the Reagan Doctrine, America was the crusader for freedom, not the guarantor of international law and order. The Reagan Doctrine, certainly in its more expansive version, subordinated the traditional bases of international order to a particular version of legitimacy by proclaiming a right of intervention against nondemocratic governments and particularly against Marxist-Leninist governments. In doing so, it went well beyond the grounds for intervention sanctioned by the traditions and practice of states. It declared that even when a state's security interests, conventionally defined, were not in jeopardy and when its support of rebel movements was not a form of counter-intervention, intervention might nevertheless be justified to overturn illegitimate governments. The latter presumably had no rights, legitimacy being defined in terms of conformity to the democratic process.

The Reagan Doctrine cast the nation in the role of extending freedom and not only of defending it, as earlier the Truman Doctrine had done. The essence of the Reagan Doctrine, again in contrast with the Truman Doctrine, was the promotion of freedom even at the risk of greater disorder. In part, the subordination of the claims of order was justified simply by invoking what were proclaimed to be the superior claims of freedom. In part, however, the response to the criticism that the Reagan Doctrine was inimi-

54   cal to the claims of order was that any real semblance of international order had long ceased to exist. International order, the argument ran, must ultimately rest on the promise and reality that the rules comprising such order will be reciprocally observed. Since our communist adversaries obeyed no law other than the law of expediency, we were held to be under no obligation to conform to the norms of the "old" order which, indifferent to internal forms of legitimacy, rested on the foundation of self-determination, sovereignty, and nonintervention. These norms were given their principal institutional expression in the UN. During the years of the Reagan administration, the relationship between the American government and the world organization reached its lowest point. The Reagan Doctrine in its various articulations reflected a thinly disguised contempt for the UN. The unilateralism that plainly characterized the doctrine was an all but formal rejection of the organization that was seen as increasingly dominated by states hostile to American interests and purposes.

Yet the Bush administration appeared to virtually reverse the outlook that informed the Reagan Doctrine. It did so by its insistence during the gulf crisis that the measures taken against Iraq have a multilateral character and that their legitimacy be based on authorizing decisions of the UN Security Council. More significantly still, it did so by virtue of the role it assigned to the UN and to the principle of collective security in the administration's vision of a new world order. That vision not only placed principal emphasis on the maintenance of law and order; in assigning to the United States the role of ensuring order, it also pledged that this role would be undertaken within the institutional constraints of the UN. This represented a striking change from the position of the preceding administration.

Equally striking was the insistence of the Bush administration on playing a role the nation was thought to have rejected a generation ago, in circumstances far less exigent than those of a generation ago. The Johnson administration intervened in Vietnam for largely the same reasons that the Bush administration intervened in the Persian Gulf. In both instances, the interest in and commitment to world order was advanced as a—if not *the*—

compelling motivation of American policy. In both instances as well, the interest in world order was considered inseparable from American security. The American intervention in Vietnam was repeatedly justified in terms of the freedom and self-determination of the South Vietnamese. Unless this could be assured in the case of South Vietnam, it was argued, the prospects for world order were slight. If these prospects were diminished, the security of the United States was correspondingly diminished. Were this country to refuse the role of policeman, the Johnson administration repeatedly contended, world order would be placed in jeopardy and with it America's security. World order, in turn, formed an undifferentiated whole, with the result that a challenge to one part of this order formed a challenge to every part. It followed, in the words of then secretary of state Dean Rusk, "We can be safe only to the extent that our total environment is safe."

It was the equation of world order with American security upon which the Johnson administration's defense of Vietnam ultimately had to stand or fall. In the end, we know, the administration failed to make that equation effective. In the context of a conflict marked by many difficulties, the argument was rejected by the nation. Yet the same contention, once considered by many as excessive, even in circumstances that gave it a substantial measure of plausibility, was widely accepted in the course of the gulf crisis, and despite the fact that circumstances were markedly, even radically, more favorable to American security than those prevailing at the time of Vietnam.

The explanation for this reversion to a role that was so widely rejected as a result of Vietnam may in part be accounted for precisely by the vast change in circumstances that had occurred. It is because the equation once drawn between American security and world order was far less compelling in 1990 than at the time of Vietnam that it acquired a new attractiveness. The fact that it was less compelling at the time of the gulf crisis also meant that it no longer entailed the risk when acted upon that it once did. Our ability to entertain an order-giving role in circumstances which permitted, or seemed to permit, the implementation of this role to

56   be undertaken without the costs it once imposed gave it a new attractiveness.

It is also the case, however, that the goals America was to pursue in the Bush administration's vision of a new world order were those that had long found support in twentieth century American diplomacy. An emphasis on the rule of law and the maintenance of order has been as pronounced as the emphasis on promoting freedom. The freedom *of* nations (self-determination) has been seen to be quite as important as the freedom *in* nations (democratic institutions). In the American view, the two have been viewed as mutually supportive, even symbiotic. If experience has shown that this is not always so, the point remains that we have persisted in believing that it is so. Certainly, Woodrow Wilson believed that it was so. It was largely what he meant by a world made "safe for democracy." Franklin Roosevelt subscribed to it. The same conviction formed an integral part of the Truman Doctrine. Even the Reagan Doctrine did not really reject it. The "disorder" sanctioned by the Reagan Doctrine can be explained by the persuasion that a satisfactory and enduring international order can be achieved only if totalitarian power is banished. A season of disorder is sanctioned so that a true system of international order can be established.

The Bush vision of a new world order, then, was not novel. Nor was the role the nation is assigned to play in that order novel. If the shift in emphasis from defending and promoting freedom to ensuring order represented a marked change when seen against the background of the past generation, this may be largely accounted for by the unexpected events that virtually transformed the international system, above all, the sudden end of the cold war. These events set the stage for what appeared to be a curious reversion to an earlier period in our history, to the period of World War I. In Bush's vision of a new world order, we witnessed a replay of sorts of Woodrow Wilson's vision of a new world order. For both, the states of the world, great and small, were to be guaranteed the same right of respect for their sovereignty and territorial integrity. For both, the peace of the world was to be maintained and democratic societies to be made safe against the threat of arbitrary power by a

universal system of collective security which would create a com-   **57**
munity of power in place of the age-old balance of power (the
threat to peace and order being considered general rather than
specific). And, of course, for both, the United States was destined
to play the role of leadership in the new world order, a role that fell
to the nation primarily because it alone had "sufficient moral
force" (Wilson) or "moral standing" (Bush) to lead the other
nations of the world.

In the manner of most historical parallels, however, this one
is far from exact. If the similarities between the two visions are
striking, the differences are scarcely less impressive. Wilson's new
world order implied, and indeed necessitated, sweeping change in
the status quo. The international system that prevailed to World
War I, with its militarism and imperialism, its great and imposed
inequalities, its secret diplomacy and its balance of power, had
resulted in the disaster of the Great War. It had to be transformed
if peace was to be preserved and democratic institutions to be
safeguarded. A just peace, the only peace that would last, required
the recasting of borders to satisfy the principle of self-determination. It also required putting an end to the system of inequality
known as colonialism, and it dictated a new diplomacy, the
effectiveness of which would rest on the power of public opinion,
which, when the necessity arose, could be supplemented by economic power. Mediated through democratic governments sharing
common purposes and interests, these forms of power, rather than
armed force, would provide the foundations of the new world
order, and the sanctions provisions of the League of Nations
covenant were designed accordingly. Wilson was not the first
American statesman to place high hopes on finding an effective
substitute for war. A century before, Jefferson had done so. But
whereas Jefferson had done so in circumstances of American
weakness, Wilson did so when the nation's power was reaching a
new level of greatness.

In all of these respects, the contrast with Bush's vision is
apparent. The new world order proclaimed by the president did
not promise or require sweeping change in the status quo. There
was little reason to believe that Bush saw either himself or the

58   nation he represented as the agent of change in the sense that
Wilson did. To be sure, it could be argued that given the changes
that had occurred in the world—the disappearance of the colonial
system and of the inequalities it sanctioned, the acceptance and
substantial realization of the principle of self-determination, and,
above all, the apparent triumph and vindication of free institutions—Bush did not feel the need for change that was evident in
Wilson's day. Even so, the point remains that for Bush the new
world order was the status quo. The equation that Wilson could
not make, even had he been disposed to do so, for fear of sacrificing
his principal bases of support, Bush was both disposed to make and
found little difficulty in making.

While the institutional mechanisms (the League of Nations
and the UN) through which the respective visions were to be
realized are similar, the distinctive means on which primary reliance was to be placed were not. The faith Wilson had in the
power of public opinion either to prevent or to defeat aggression
was lost; and the same must be said of the confidence he placed in
the efficacy of economic sanctions. To an extent that would
undoubtedly have shocked Wilson, Bush accepted and indeed
embraced many of the presuppositions of the old diplomacy, particularly the reliance on force, in proclaiming his new world order.
The dream of banishing aggression persisted but the principal
means for doing so were those which Wilson had largely excluded
from his new world order.

Wilson's vision remained just that. His vision assumed a
peace that could not possibly be gained in the wake of a terrible
war—one so destructive of the very conditions indispensable to
democratic development—save by a victor possessed of truly overweening power and ready, if necessary, to impose such a peace.
Despite the favorable position of the United States at the close of
World War I, these conditions were not even approximated (as
they were at the close of World War II). Yet in the absence of a
peace that left all of the major states satisfied and democratic (or
well on their way to becoming so), it was difficult to see how, even
under Wilsonian assumptions, the great institutional mechanism
for fashioning and employing a community of power, and thus

guaranteeing peace, could work. On the other hand, given a peace that satisfied all of the major states, now either democratic or on a democratic course, there would be no real need of a League of Nations to give expression to a community of power. For either the occasions requiring the use of such power would not arise or, if they exceptionally did, the remaining democratic states—with or without a League—would be quite capable of dealing with the errant government.

The Wilsonian vision could not be sought primarily through the League of Nations. The effectiveness of the system of collective security Wilson had championed depended on a community of interest and power which did not exist and which could not be called into existence by incantation. In the absence of such community, Wilson was faced with the choice between attempting to change the international system or adapting to it. Changing the international system, that is, attempting directly to create what did not exist, required a degree of power well beyond America's capabilities at the time and a commitment to the use of power well beyond America's will. Even had Wilson believed in the need of such a commitment, and urged its acceptance by the nation, he still would have had to persuade the nation that America's security depended on making the commitment. This Wilson would not do because he did not believe it to be true. Nor is it apparent that had he believed it to be true he could have gained the public support required for so momentous a transformation of policy.

The alternative course of adapting to the system rather than attempting to transform it also required a break from the nation's past. Championed by Wilson's Republican critics, Theodore Roosevelt, Henry Cabot Lodge, and Elihu Root, this course entailed a victors' alliance, an alliance of democratic states designed to guarantee the territorial settlement and to ensure a favorable balance of power in the postwar period. But Wilson, despite the treaty of guarantee he concluded at Versailles with France and Great Britain (later quietly dropped), would not seriously consider following this course (one that did not preclude American participation in a League of Nations but that would have altered the significance of this participation). He would not do so given his

60   aversion to the old diplomacy and its obsession with equilibrating power by means of alliances and, when necessity arose, the use of armed force. There had to be another way to guarantee peace rather than the way of a balance of power that left peace at the mercy of the competitive process—one which had inevitably resulted in the destruction of all past balances.

Thus America emerged victorious from a war that was to have issued in a new world order without having committed its power either to the achievement of a new order or to the effective maintenance of the old order. While the American role in the world was not the same after the war as it had been before, neither was it the role that Wilson had cast. The interwar period was anything but a time when, in the words Wilson had once used, America exercised "the infinite privilege of fulfilling her destiny and saving the world." [1]

When the United States finally committed its great power to the task of international order following World War II, it did not do so on behalf of the system of collective security that succeeded the League of Nations. That system, given the emerging hostility between the Soviet Union and the West, was stillborn. The community of power and purpose that an effective collective security system presupposes, but cannot simply create, disappeared with the defeat of the Axis states. In its stead emerged a conflict that could be managed only by pursuing the age-old strategy of alliance and the balance of power.

In the brief period before the cold war dispensation became apparent, however, the new world order was equated with the international security organization established by the victorious allies—above all, the United States—in the closing stages of the war. It is useful to recall that the UN was initially conceived as a collective security organization in name only. In practice, it was intended to be an alliance of the victorious great powers of World War II, an alliance principally directed against the threat presumably posed by a revival of German and Japanese aggression. In retrospect, that intent may seem inexplicable, but it did not appear so to most in the circumstances of the last year of the war when the charter was drafted. At that time, the great task was

believed to be that of preventing history from repeating itself. **61**
Only the continued cooperation of the principal powers that had
fought Germany and Japan, it was thought, could ensure that this
would not happen. The charter of the UN was seen as the instrument for preserving that cooperation.

The preeminent position thus accorded the victorious great
powers in the charter was justified in part on this basis. In part,
though, it simply rested on the familiar claim that power must be
commensurate with responsibility. There was little that was novel
in the principle of a great power directorate presiding over the
peace and order of the world. That principle had been a foundation of the settlement following the Napoleonic wars in the early
nineteenth century. Nor had it been absent from the plan of a new
world order worked out at Versailles following World War I. However great the emphasis placed on the equality of states, they were
not equal in the plan of the covenant. The great power members of
the League of Nations enjoyed a distinctive position of power and
responsibility, one reflected in the provisions respecting the membership and functions of the League Council. Even so, this position paled in significance when set alongside that accorded the
principal victors of World War II by the UN Charter. The charter
represented, as supporters and critics alike agreed, the apotheosis
of power. "If the Security Council decided that Utopia must
surrender the whole or part of her territory to Arcadia," one critic
of the charter wrote at the time, "the decision is not only binding
upon the parties but all the members of the UN are pledged to
assist in carrying it into effect."[2] The relevant provisions of the
charter confirm this still startling conclusion. Those provisions
conferred what amounted to an unlimited discretion in matters of
peace and security on the great powers in their role as permanent
members of the Security Council, provided only that they
remained united in outlook.

What was novel about the new world order championed by
the American government at the end of World War II was the
length to which it carried the principle of great power supremacy.
That this principle was to be given so predominant a role only
during a relatively brief period of postwar transition, as was occa-

62   sionally intimated by the Roosevelt administration, strained credulity. Quite apart from the difficulty so basic a change in the
charter necessarily would have entailed, the position accorded the
great powers responded to the belief, held by the president on
down, that perhaps the most important reason for the League of
Nations' failure was that the major states, those bearing the
greatest responsibility for peace, had not been given sufficient
power in the covenant. That this reading of the experience with
collective security in the interwar period was plainly at odds with
the historical record appeared irrelevant. The League had failed to
keep the peace, the familiar argument ran, because the great
powers had not been given a sufficiently dominant role and, of
course, because one great power, the United States, had played no
role at all.

The provisions of the UN Charter, which were designed to
prevent a recurrence of the interwar experience, may be better
understood, however, as reflecting the American government's
determination not to agree to any security arrangements that
would constitute, or that would even be seen as constituting, a
marked departure from the past. There was little in the charter to
upset those who wished to continue a policy that avoided alliances
and interventions outside the Western Hemisphere and that preserved a complete independence of action. The essential characteristics of an isolationist policy might well be preserved despite
membership in the UN. Although the charter consecrated as
never before the principle of great power supremacy, and conferred
on the mighty an almost unlimited discretion in matters of peace
and security, provided that they could agree on a given course of
action, it obligated them to nothing in the way of guaranteeing the
political independence and territorial integrity of the member
states of the organization.

The veto power possessed by each of the permanent members
thus ensured that in matters of collective enforcement the United
States retained the same freedom of action—or inaction—that it
had always insisted upon in the past. It was with this understanding that the Senate accepted the charter. There was no repetition
in 1945 of the fight that had been waged in 1919, because, among

other reasons, there was plainly no reason to assume that in **63** joining the UN this country had in any way compromised its freedom to determine the circumstances in which it would employ force. The right of veto, which formed the essential precondition of American membership in the UN, also effectively ended a dispute that had gone on for more than a generation. It did so, however, by vindicating the position taken by Wilson's great senatorial adversary, Henry Cabot Lodge; the power of veto was the functional equivalent, and indeed more, of what Lodge had insisted on in 1919.

In retrospect, there is no little irony in the fate of the principal criticism that was initially directed against the charter. This criticism was not so much that the system of the charter would not work but that it would work only with respect to the smaller powers. No enforcement measures could be taken against the great powers possessing permanent seats on the Security Council, given the right of veto enjoyed by each. The enemy powers of World War II apart—states that according to Article 107 of the charter could be dealt with at will by any member of the organization that had been at war with them—only the small powers remained as prospective objects of the enforcement measures provided for in the charter. A collective security organization limited to taking enforcement actions against only the smaller powers, the criticism ran, was hardly a sufficient guarantee for the maintenance of international peace and security.

What critics once viewed as a grave defect was seen during the gulf crisis almost as a virtue. In a world that no longer appeared threatened by great power conflicts arising from age-old motives of territorial expansion, there remained only the threat posed by smaller powers whose aspirations and state of development had yet to be reconciled with the norms of a more conventional statecraft. In this world, the UN, under American leadership, was once again found to express the community of power that Wilson had aspired in vain to find in the League. This was so because American leadership was virtually unchallenged by any other great power. What many saw as an emergent global community of power was inseparable from America's new-found hegemonial position.

64   In the world of the late 1940s, however, there clearly was no such community of power. Although America's position was in many respects even more ascendant than it was in the gulf crisis, it was not unchallenged. The onset of the long conflict with the Soviet Union, a conflict which made irrelevant the order of the charter, of necessity gave rise to efforts at creating a limited community of power. These efforts, occurring roughly over the period 1947–1952, resulted in the great transformation of American foreign policy. In undertaking to create with the nations of Western Europe a partial community of power for the purpose of countering the power of the Soviet Union, the United States abandoned its historic policy of isolation—something it had not done by participating in the UN. Whereas membership in the world organization committed the nation to very little that broke from historic tradition, the creation of the Western alliance broke from the entirety of that tradition, centered as it was on the avoidance of entanglement—above all, permanent entanglement—in Europe's politics. In a period of only several years, American foreign policy shifted from the new politics of collective security—which President Roosevelt characterized in his last address to Congress as "the end of the system of unilateral action, exclusive alliances, spheres of influence, and balances of power"— to the old politics that had supposedly been left behind in establishing the UN.[3]

This reversion to the old politics, though not easy, was in some measure facilitated by the way the change was perceived. An embrace of the old politics was frequently characterized as a realization of the new politics. Thus the Senate hearings on the North Atlantic Treaty Organization (NATO) were marked by the care with which the treaty was distinguished from the traditional military alliance, which was, as Senator Arthur Vandenberg noted, a "partnership for power" rather than, as was the case with NATO, a "partnership for peace."[4] A State Department memorandum on the differences between NATO and traditional military alliances sought to distinguish between the two by noting that alliances "were designed to advance the respective nationalistic interests of the parties, and provided for joint military action if one of the parties in pursuit of such objectives became involved in war." NATO, however, was a pure application of collective security: "It is directed against no one; it is directed solely against aggression. It seeks not to influence any shifting 'balance of power' but to strengthen the 'balance of principle.'"[5]

In time, a balance of power diplomacy based in the main on the Western alliance came to be accepted for what it was. Yet what it was did in fact go beyond the vital task of balancing power against power. Although the Western alliance was plainly directed against a specific adversary, it not only formed a community of power but of ideals as well. What came to be known as the "free world" had as its essential core the nations that made up the Western alliance. The great achievement of American foreign policy in the postwar period, and the principal achievement of the policy of containment, was the creation of a partial, though not a universal, community of power and value.

The postwar order was an order inseparable from containment. With some exaggeration, it may even be seen as the order of containment. Although this order brought a remarkable measure of security, peace, and prosperity to the nations of the Western alliance, we were never quite satisfied with the policy that made these results possible. Conservatives criticized containment from the outset for being too defensive and for failing to hold out the solid prospect of bringing the great contest with the Soviet Union to an early and victorious end. Indeed, until the eve of the Soviet Union's sudden collapse as a superpower, the Right continued to insist, even more emphatically than in earlier years, that containment, if continued, would issue in catastrophe. Liberals, too, though for the opposite reason, came increasingly to believe that the pursuit of containment would lead to disaster. From the time of Vietnam, those who had once been containment's strongest supporters came more and more to equate that policy with the excesses that had led to the nation's involvement in Southeast Asia. Caught between these attacks from the Right and the Left, containment survived only in practice. Even the startling and unexpected vindication of that policy at the close of the 1980s has

66   apparently not been sufficient to rehabilitate it in the nation's memory.

The policy that essentially defined the American position in the postwar world finally came to an end. Containment had come to a close, having played a vital role in the creation of conditions which provided in turn for its demise. Those circumstances, for the first time in a half century, released the United States from the need to pursue a balance of power policy. Although the nation might pursue a policy that sought the creation and maintenance of regional balances, it would do so from choice rather than from necessity. In the absence of a great power challenge, there was no compelling need to pursue such a course. The equation established at the outset of the cold war among order, freedom, and security had been broken. The freedom to turn inward and to devote a new attention to domestic purposes was greater than it had been since the 1930s. It was also the case, though, that the circumstances which made this new-found freedom possible also made it possible to assume a role that the nation's leadership, with few exceptions, had aspired to play in this century: that of giving order to the world. For the third time in this century, a future beckoned in which this role was to be undertaken within the framework of a system of collective security. For the first time in this century, however, circumstances held out a promise of success for this role that was not apparent on earlier occasions.

The peace that Woodrow Wilson's vision of world order assumed, but did not possess, appeared to have been substantially realized. The world, though still far from democratic, had been made safe for democracy. The foundation that Wilson considered indispensable to a lasting structure of peace and security had been laid. The triumph of free institutions had justified, if not fulfilled, the expectations of America's World War I president.

The position of American primacy that Wilson's vision of world order assumed, but did not really possess, had also been achieved. Moreover, it was attended by a will to use the nation's military power that was very far from apparent then (as, indeed, it had been less than apparent in the post-Vietnam period). Wilson did not believe reliance on military power to be necessary for the

success of collective security. For such success, economic power   **67**
and the force of public opinion would prove sufficient. Experience
was to disabuse Wilson's successors of this persuasion. What experience did not disabuse them of was Wilson's belief that collective
security would be distinguished by the ease with which it might be
effectively implemented. While the Bush administration was
quite prepared to use means which its predecessor would have
shrunk from using, it too was persuaded that future efforts in
collective security, like the effort that was undertaken in the
Persian Gulf, would be distinguished by the ease with which the
system was implemented. The military interventions that might
yet have to be undertaken, despite the object lesson made of
Iraq, were expected to entail a quite modest price in blood and
treasure.

This persistence of belief in the ease with which collective
security may be implemented responded to the deeply ingrained
American habit of willing grand ends through only modest means.
Though the means President Bush employed against Iraq were
anything but modest, they were in fact very modest when measured in terms of American casualties and financial costs to the
nation. Moreover, the costs of sustaining the new world order
would have to remain modest if it were to have a promising future.
There was nothing in the gulf experience which set aside the
lesson that public support for a foreign policy requiring substantial
sacrifice could only be assured provided it could be demonstrated
that vital security interests of the nation are at stake. Role would
have to be effectively equated with security, and security given a
conventional meaning. The failure to make this equation effectively provided the principal cause of the opposition to the intervention in Vietnam. So, too, the new world order would be
doomed unless its implementation avoided the costs of Vietnam.

Whether it would prove possible to enforce the new world
order at only modest cost largely depended on whether the experience of the Persian Gulf War established a pattern for the future.
Should it establish such a pattern, America's persisting technological advantages would ensure small casualties, while low financial
cost would result from the continued willingness of others—above

68   all, our principal allies—to pay for America's order-maintaining role. Even if the first condition could be safely assumed, the second could not. Burden sharing on behalf of the new world order is unlikely to prove a less contentious arrangement than burden sharing in support of the old order of containment was. Since those asked to share the new burden might feel less compelled to do so, it could prove to be far more contentious. The thought might not be long in forming that the United States was using the center to order the periphery, while using the periphery (above all, the Middle East) to maintain its influence over the center.

The new world order also rested on the likelihood of the cooperation of the permanent members of the Security Council. Without that cooperation, the United States would be deprived of the legitimacy it had enjoyed in the gulf crisis. Whether that cooperation would be forthcoming, however, was very uncertain. The instability that marks the domestic politics of the new Russian state and China might well deprive the United States, in a future crisis, of the support it enjoyed in the Security Council in 1990–1991. Whether it could rely, in that event, on the endorsement of the Western alliance is by no means assured. Despite alliance support of the American-led action against Iraq, it was by no means apparent that future actions could be assured comparable support. The alliance support given in the gulf crisis was given, after all, in the context of UN support. In a future crisis, assuming that it arose in the developing world, an absence of the latter might well give to the former the appearance of renewed north-south confrontation. Whatever their other reservations might be, it seems safe to assume that at least some alliance members will strongly desire to avoid giving this appearance. That desire might even lead them to withhold endorsement of an American-led initiative.

★   ★   ★

The fate of the new world order is necessarily speculative. Yet it is striking that, under the Bush administration, the United States has returned to the vision—Woodrow Wilson's vision—with which it began its long odyssey at the outset of this century, only this time attended by a willingness to use means which Wilson **69** himself had disavowed. The extent to which the promissory notes of the new world order will have to be redeemed in the future remains unclear. What does seem clear, however, is that the principal threats to order after the gulf war stem not from the prospect of naked territorial aggression against which the new world order is primarily directed, but from the disintegration of existing states as a result of the insistence of peoples on self-determination. The great problem that confronted Woodrow Wilson, and that he sought to address by proclaiming that every people should have its own state, also confronts George Bush. The new world order, however, does not address this prospective danger. It is, for all intents and purposes, the order of the status quo.

PART TWO

The Gulf War: An Autopsy

CHAPTER 5

The Costs of the War

I n late February 1991, following America's military victory over Iraq in the Persian Gulf War, President Bush stood at the height of his popularity, obtaining near unanimous approval ratings from the American public. His handling of the crisis was widely praised as masterful. He had led an unprecedented international coalition to war against a tyrant whose every action confirmed a reputation for villainy. Over the doubts and hesitations of many at home and abroad, he had succeeded in winning the support of both the UN Security Council and the U.S. Congress for resolutions authorizing the use of "all necessary means" to expel Iraq from Kuwait after January 15, 1991.[1] He had successfully appealed to the memory of one war (World War II) as defining the nature of the nation's current struggle, and he had rooted out and confounded the discomfiting memories of another war (Vietnam) that had shaken the nation's resolve and left it bitterly divided. He had triumphantly proclaimed a new world order.

Characterized in advance by Secretary of Defense Dick Cheney as "one of the largest land assaults of modern times,"[2] the military victory was nevertheless won with only 148 American fatalities. With but few exceptions, public opinion had anticipated a far worse result from hostilities. It had heard with alarm the stories that the Pentagon had placed special rush orders for over 16,000 body bags in preparation for the day of battle. Up until the eve of the decision to launch the ground war, it had told the pollsters in lopsided majorities that it hoped that the air campaign against Iraq would be given more time. A ground war, the public

74   felt instinctively, would be far costlier for the United States than the air campaign, and would in all probability prompt the use of chemical weapons against American forces. Hoping to avoid another Vietnam, with its frightful toll in American lives, yet believing also that the war in Vietnam had been partly lost by division at home, the public concluded that there was no alternative to supporting the president, even as it feared the outcome. Against the background of these fears, the overwhelming victory won by American military forces, together with its small cost in American lives, induced euphoria in public opinion.

The gulf war was highly unusual not only in its small cost in American lives; in the aftermath of the conflict, it turned out that nearly all of the extraordinary financial costs of the gulf operation had been borne by allied states. This, too, was unexpected. In the days leading up to the war, critics of the administration had complained repeatedly over the sheer unfairness of asking the United States to assume a military role to vindicate interests in the Persian Gulf of far greater moment to America's allies in Europe and Japan than to the United States. In the aftermath of the war, some observers argued that the United States might actually have turned a profit on the operation.[3] For the United States, this was the most unusual of wars, and for the American people, it entailed little of the suffering and privation normally attendant on armed conflict.

Such was not the case for America's adversary. Iraq suffered grievously from the war. Though estimates of Iraqi military fatalities remained highly uncertain in the aftermath of the conflict, the unofficial Pentagon estimate was that 100,000 Iraqi soldiers lost their lives in the intensive bombardment of frontline Iraqi positions. (Some observers put the total at between 100,000 and 150,000, others at between 25,000 and 50,000.) *

---

* The number of Iraqi military casualties remains shrouded in obscurity. The Defense Intelligence Agency estimated that 100,00 Iraqi soldiers may have been killed during the war, but noted that the "error factor" in this estimate was 50 percent or higher. Incredibly, the DIA also estimated 300,000 wounded, an estimate that is totally inconsistent with battlefield reports and may be safely attributed to methodological incompetence on the DIA's part. (If there

Though direct Iraqi civilian fatalities from American air
attacks probably numbered less than 5,000, and may have been
considerably lower, the indirect effects of the American bombing

---

were a three to one ratio between wounded and killed in past wars, the agency's
analysts seem to have reasoned, a similar ratio must have held in the Iraq war,
despite the obvious differences in operational conditions.)

The Central Intelligence Agency (CIA) and DIA estimated before the
war that about 550,000 Iraqis were deployed in the southern theater at the
time of the allied air offensive. It now seems well established that this
estimate—which assumed that Iraqi divisions were at full strength—was
considerably exaggerated. According to a report in *Newsday* (Patrick J.
Sloyan, "U.S. Faced Fewer Iraqis; Casualty Estimates Also Being Lowered,"
January 24, 1992), a new administration account of the war to be submitted to
Congress will estimate that 380,000 Iraqis were deployed when the air war
began, that only 200,000 remained at the outset of the ground offensive, and
that 87,000 were taken prisoner. Casualty estimates are still being debated
inside the administration, but the principal source of Sloyan's report, Lt. Gen.
Charles Horner, said that 25,000 was a "reasonable" number for Iraqi dead.

Because most Iraqis were likely killed inside their collapsing bunkers,
which became instant burial sites, prisoner interrogation was an indispensable
method for acquiring a picture of the unfolding of the war, including desertion
rates and enemy casualties. It is not clear, however, whether such interroga-
tions were undertaken on any serious scale. At the time of the war, public
comments by U.S. civilian and military officials stressed their disinterest in
the question of Iraqi casualties. Their attitude derived primarily, no doubt,
from the potential moral and political embarrassment over a very high number
of Iraqi dead. Given the war plan that the United States embraced and the
then prevailing estimates of Iraqi strength, senior officials likely assumed that a
serious investigation would yield a high number and preferred that the question remain a mystery. In May 1991, General Powell, when asked about the
number of Iraqi casualties, replied, "I don't have a clue and I don't really plan
to undertake any real effort to try and find out." (Quoted in R. Jeffrey Smith,
"Iraqi Casualty Story Begins to Emerge; Both Sides in Gulf War Reluctant to
Address Sensitive Subject," *The Washington Post*, September 13, 1991.)

Powell's attitude is not defensible. Even if the difficulties of estimating
Iraqi casualties are taken into account, it is not a matter of indifference
whether the United States develops war fighting strategies that are disdainful
of such traditional standards as proportionality, military necessity, and economy of force. The number of Iraqi casualties is relevant to, even if not
necessarily determinative of, the inquiry into whether the United States
observed those standards in the gulf conflict, just as it is relevant to the
question of the kind of war strategies the American military ought to employ in
the future. From the insistence that the United States does not know and does
not care about the number of Iraqi casualties, it is but a short step to the
conclusion that these traditional standards are irrelevant as well.

76   on civilian life were very serious indeed. Air attacks on electrical grids, power plants, transportation bottlenecks, and communications facilities threw the country, at least temporarily, back into the preindustrial age. In the absence of electricity, sewage treatment plants and hospitals were incapable of functioning, and fresh water was made generally unavailable. A grave public health crisis ensued, with widespread outbreaks of cholera, typhoid, and other diseases. A UN team dispatched to Iraq in the immediate aftermath of the war declared conditions there to be "near apocalyptic." Iraq, the UN report said, "has, for some time to come, been relegated to a preindustrial age, but with all the disabilities of postindustrial dependency on an intensive use of energy and technology." In May 1991, a group of specialists from Harvard predicted that "at least 170,000 children under five years of age will die in the coming year from the delayed effects of the gulf crisis."*

---

* Patrick E. Tyler, "U.S. Officials Believe Iraq Will Take Years to Rebuild," *The New York Times*, June 3, 1991. See also Barton Gellman, "Storm Damage in the Persian Gulf," *The Washington Post National Weekly Edition*, July 8–14, 1991, pp. 6–7. See also *Public Health in Iraq After the Gulf War* (Harvard Study Team Report, mimeo, May 1991). The Harvard team insisted that its estimates were conservative and that, "in all probability, the actual number of deaths of children under five will be much higher." "The immediate cause of death in most cases," the report held, "will be waterborne infectious disease in combination with severe malnutrition." The latter factor is "primarily due to severe food shortages and a consequent tenfold or more increase in the price of food." The sharp increase in the incidence of waterborne diseases was the "result of the destruction of electrical generating plants in the gulf war and the consequent failure of water purification and sewage treatment systems." Such diseases would be treatable if Iraq's medical system were functioning; the study team, however, found that the state of medical care was desperate and—unless conditions changed substantially—would continue to deteriorate. It identified the collapse of electrical generating capacity as a "crucial factor in this public health catastrophe" (pp. 1–3).

    A subsequent study team sent to Iraq between August 23 and September 5, 1991, reported projections for child mortality consistent with the earlier findings of the Harvard team. See *Health and Welfare in Iraq After the Gulf Crisis: An In-Depth Assessment* (International Study Team, mimeo, October 1991). The International Study Team noted that "because of the nature and sequence of health-influencing events occurring over the past 12 months (sanctions, war, civil disturbances), it is nearly impossible to separate the effect of one event from the others."

In addition to the vast human costs that followed directly from the use of American military power against Iraq, the gulf crisis was also associated with an ecological disaster in Kuwait, when retreating Iraqi forces set fire to over half of Kuwait's oil wells. It also set in motion the large-scale flight and expulsion of refugees. Saddam Hussein's invasion of Kuwait in August 1990 provoked the flight of some 380,000 Kuwaitis from their homeland; over a million Egyptians, Indians, and other nationalities who had worked in Iraq and Kuwait before the war also fled from the area, mostly through Jordan. Saudi Arabia in effect expelled approximately eight hundred thousand to a million Yemenis from its kingdom soon after the outbreak of the war. When Kuwait was liberated, another wave of expulsions followed; Palestinians, who had played a major role in running Kuwaiti institutions before the war, but who were suspected of having collaborated with Saddam Hussein in the aftermath of the invasion, were either refused reentry to Kuwait or threatened with expulsion. Up to 400,000 Palestinians had lived in Kuwait before the war; in the aftermath of the conflict, the Kuwaitis made clear their determination to rid themselves of much of the Palestinian presence.[4]

The largest and most dramatic flight of people, which took place in Iraq itself, was comprised of some two million Kurds who fled to the borders of Turkey and Iran after Saddam Hussein suppressed their rebellion. Unlike the other flights of people that occurred as a result of the crisis and the war, this was one in which American opinion took a keen though horrified interest, since the United States might be held indirectly responsible for it. Before and during the war, President Bush had called upon the Iraqi people to take matters into their own hands and depose Saddam Hussein. When the uprisings of the Shi'a and Kurdish peoples occurred, however, the administration looked upon them with apprehension. If successful, the risings portended the breakup of the Iraqi state, and in a manner that might seriously jeopardize American interests. Saudi Arabia warned of the possibility that a rump Shi'a state in the south would inevitably look to Teheran for its own protection, and hence extend Iranian power and influence in a manner threatening to the conservative regimes of the gulf. In

78   the north, the possibility of an independent Kurdistan alarmed
both Turkey and Syria, important coalition partners in the gulf
war. The potential for "Lebanonization"—interminable conflict
among rival sectarian and ethnic groups, spilling beyond Iraq's
boundaries—seemed great.

Under these circumstances, the administration announced a
policy of nonintervention in Iraq's civil war. A warning issued by
President Bush on March 13, 1991, against the use of Iraqi
helicopters in the civil war was effectively withdrawn on March
26. Having portrayed Saddam Hussein as evil incarnate for some
months, the administration now clearly wished that he would be
successful in crushing the rebellion, or at least in preserving the
Iraqi state intact. (It then hoped for a military coup against him.)
In justifying its policy of nonintervention, it appealed to the very
principle of international society—the sanctity of state sovereignty—that it had championed in the war to liberate Kuwait. It
insisted that the UN resolutions that had authorized military
action against the Iraqi occupation of Kuwait provided no mandate to intervene in Iraq's civil war. To go beyond these resolutions
not only risked breaking the international consensus; it also con-
jured up the prospect of an interminable involvement by American forces in ethnic and religious fighting that, as the president
said, had gone on "for ages."

These were weighty objections to a policy of intervention. It
was nevertheless difficult to maintain them in the face of the vast
human agony that now unfolded in Iraq. As Saddam Hussein
regrouped his main Republican Guard forces, two to three divisions of which had been spared at the last moment by the American announcement of a temporary cease-fire, he moved against
the Shi'a in the south and the Kurds in the north with extraordinary brutality, inducing in the north an unprecedented movement
of nearly two million Kurdish refugees to the borders of Turkey and
Iran, and a flight of hundreds of thousands of Shi'a to the marsh-
lands of southern Iraq. It was difficult to deny that the United
States played a major role in setting these events in motion. The
administration might find shelter from critics behind the legal
shield of nonintervention; at the same time, it was not unreason-

able to read the president's previous call for Saddam Hussein's **79**
overthrow as a pledge of American support and protection, and his
subsequent stance of nonintervention as a betrayal of that pledge.
Shivering on their bleak mountaintops, and dying at a rate of one
to two thousand a day, every Kurd interviewed by the Western
media thought so.

The president had portrayed the struggle over Kuwait as a
stark and simple conflict of good versus evil, and he had dwelt
often on the atrocities Iraqi forces committed in Kuwait. To stand
aside while atrocities on a far greater scale were being committed
within Iraq, in circumstances for which the United States was
partially responsible (as it had not been for the previous atrocities
in Kuwait), threw into grave doubt the moral basis of the American effort. After overwhelming pressure from both European allies
and domestic critics, the administration finally consented to steps
to provide humanitarian aid to Kurdish refugees in Turkey and to
create protective enclaves guarded by American forces in northern
Iraq. The limited steps it finally took, however, did not erase the
memory of its conduct in late March and early April. The *real-
politik* of the spring appeared suddenly jarring in the aftermath of
the moralism of the winter. The United States, it came to be
widely said, had won the war but lost the peace. And there were
intimations that it had lost its soul.

CHAPTER 6

The Justification
for the War

The preceding brief account of the immediate consequences of the war provides a point of departure for a reconsideration of the Bush administration's conduct during the crisis and the war. It insistently raises two broad questions: Should the United States have gone to war? Having gone to war, should it have adopted the aims that it did? The questions may be rephrased, and considered more pointedly, by asking, first, whether war was the only way to vindicate the interests threatened by Iraq's invasion; second, whether the ends or objectives the administration sought to achieve by going to war against Saddam Hussein were proportionate to the devastation and misery that ensued directly or indirectly from its course of action; and third, whether the decision to use force on such a scale created, where none before existed, obligations to impose a pacification that would have avoided or mitigated the human agony that unfolded in Iraq after the war.

The justification the president offered for America's conduct stressed the theme of necessity. The gulf war, the president insisted, was not a war the United States wanted, but one, on the contrary, that it made extraordinary diplomatic efforts to avoid. The desire to avoid war, however, necessarily fell short of an abandonment of the principles on which any durable peace might be built. If Saddam Hussein's aggression against Kuwait were to succeed, or otherwise bring him profit of any kind, it would constitute a threat to world order, regional security, and the global economy.

The threat to world order was based on the inadmissibility of a larger state swallowing up a smaller one, not only or even primarily because of its immediate consequences but because of the signal it would send "to actual and potential despots around the world."[1] "Every use of force unchecked is an invitation to further aggression. Every act of aggression unpunished strikes a blow against the rule of law—and strengthens the forces of chaos and lawlessness that, ultimately, threaten us all."[2] This example, if once allowed, would throw the world back into the chaos of the 1930s. It would eclipse "the bright promise of the post–Cold War era" and replace it with "new dangers, new disorders, and a far less peaceful future."[3] The choice was between a descent into anarchy and a new world order "where the rule of law, not the law of the jungle, governs the conduct of nations."[4]

The threat to regional security was equally ominous. "While might makes right is bad policy anywhere," Secretary Baker observed, "it is especially dangerous in the Middle East." Were Saddam's aggression to become the wave of the future in the region, it would be a disastrous blow to the peace process. "The prospects for a just and lasting peace between Israel and its Arab neighbors will be shattered if he prevails."[5]

The threat to regional security was closely linked to the threat to the global economy. The world community had to "prevent an individual clearly bent on regional domination from establishing a chokehold on the world's economic lifeline." The crisis, Secretary Baker held, "is not about increases in the price of a gallon of gas at the local service station. It is not just a narrow question of the flow of oil from Kuwait and Iraq. It is rather about a dictator who, acting alone and unchallenged, could strangle the global economic order, determining by fiat whether we all enter a recession or even the darkness of a depression."[6]

Virtually from the outset of the crisis, the administration argued that America's stake in world order, regional security, and the global economy could only be vindicated if Saddam Hussein was to leave Kuwait without condition. This became the marker that would demonstrate success or failure in the enterprise, the *sine qua non* without which all else would be jeopardized. Any-

82   thing less than full compliance with all UN resolutions would constitute failure and would gravely damage each of the interests and values the administration invoked.

The link the administration sought to establish between Iraq's unconditional withdrawal from Kuwait and the values and interests to which it appealed was a crucial feature of its position. A second crucial feature of the administration's position was the assumption that time was the enemy of the United States and that the crisis had to be brought to a quick resolution. Six main arguments were invoked in support of this view, most of which were detailed in the president's address to the nation announcing the onset of hostilities:

1. Economic sanctions, though effective in stopping all Iraqi oil exports and most of its imports, "showed no signs of accomplishing their objective." [7] That objective was not the punishment of Iraq as such; it was its unconditional withdrawal from Kuwait.

2. If the United States gave Saddam Hussein time, there would be nothing left of Kuwait. "While the world waited," President Bush observed, "Saddam Hussein systematically raped, pillaged, and plundered a tiny nation, no threat to his own. He subjected the people of Kuwait to unspeakable atrocities—and among those maimed and murdered, innocent children." [8]

3. The longer the crisis dragged on, the more likely it was that Saddam Hussein would acquire nuclear weapons. Given that "this brutal dictator will do anything, will use any weapon, will commit any outrage, no matter how many innocents must suffer," this was a danger that argued for an early war. [9]

4. The longer the crisis dragged on, the more damage would be done to "the fragile economies of the Third World, the emerging democracies of Eastern Europe, to the entire world including to our own economy." [10]

5. The longer the crisis dragged on, the greater the likelihood that Saddam Hussein could weaken the forces arrayed against him. The administration was circumspect in characterizing this danger, since it could only do so by questioning the motives or staying power of states it wished to maintain in the coalition. Outside

critics were more specific. They pointed to the danger that either **83** the Soviet Union or France would break from the international consensus and support a negotiated settlement that would allow Saddam Hussein to claim a victory. Down the road, sanctions would inevitably give way to negotiations, however disguised, which in turn would confer prestige on Saddam Hussein and shake all American-aligned governments in the region to their foundations. In the event of a perceived American failure, Henry Kissinger testified, "every moderate country in the Middle East would be gravely weakened. . . . Several Gulf states could not survive it. Egypt, Morocco, and even Turkey would face a tide of radicalism and fundamentalism." [11]

6. Finally, time was against the United States simply by virtue of the size of the forces it had committed to Saudi Arabia. Though President Bush did not mention this consideration in his January 16, 1991, address to the nation announcing the initiation of hostilities, everyone realized that the president's prior decision on November 8, 1990, to increase American forces to between four and five hundred thousand troops created urgent time pressures to bring the crisis to a decision. It was open to argument whether a force of 250,000 troops could remain in and around Saudi Arabia indefinitely, but there was little question that a force double that size could not do so. Given the administration's repeated declarations that it would accept nothing less than Iraq's unconditional fulfillment of all UN resolutions, it could not withdraw even parts of this greatly enlarged force in the event of partial or otherwise incomplete fulfillment without suffering a severe blow to its prestige.

The assumption that only Iraq's unconditional withdrawal from Kuwait would constitute an acceptable solution to the crisis, together with the conviction that time was an enemy, formed the basis of the administration's justification for threatening war against Iraq. The failure of Saddam Hussein to submit to this threat thus threw the responsibility for the subsequent calamities of the war squarely on his shoulders. It was Saddam Hussein who really began the war with his invasion of Kuwait on August 2,

84   1990; and it was Saddam Hussein who refused to budge from his position even after explicit warnings that his failure to do so "would be a certain calamity for the people of Iraq." [12] He was duly warned again and again.

The basic principles for which the United States went to war, according to the administration, made it equally imperative to fight a war limited to the liberation of Kuwait. The United States was the leading and indispensable partner in an international coalition; it could not simultaneously rely on this international consensus for the legal and moral authority to go to war against Iraq and then undertake a war that flouted the consensus. A war aimed at imposing an American occupation on Iraq, reconstructing the Iraqi government, and thus massively intervening in Iraq's internal affairs, according to the administration, would have exposed the United States to the charge of a grave and radical contradiction in its policy that no administration could willingly incur.

At the same time, the administration made no secret of the fact that this reluctance to strike at Baghdad, or even to offer limited support to the Kurdish and Shi'a rebellions which broke out after the temporary ceasefire, was based preeminently on domestic considerations. So, too, was the strategy the United States adopted in waging the war. From the moment when force became a realistic possibility, the president made it clear that the use of American force, if it came, would be sudden, massive, and decisive. Such a war plan not only corresponded with the advice Bush received from military leaders, it was also the only one possible if he was to satisfy the two conditions that had to be observed to sustain public support—the minimization of American casualties and a rapid conclusion to the war allowing American troops to return home.

These two conditions were heavily influenced by the memory of Vietnam. The war in Southeast Asia had shown that a protracted war that entailed substantial American casualties over time would become deeply unpopular at home. Though the president declared, in the course of the crisis, that "no price" was too great to achieve Iraq's withdrawal from Kuwait, his declaration was not to be taken literally. He understood all too well that the American people did put a price on such matters, and that domestic support would vary inversely with the size of American casualties and the length of the war.

These two conditions—minimizing American casualties and avoiding protracted engagements—were of fundamental importance in determining American war strategy and war aims. The former meant that the military would be allowed to destroy through air raids virtually any target—whether in the Kuwaiti theater or deep within Iraq itself—whose destruction might aid the immediate war effort. The latter meant that American war aims would consist of driving the Iraqis from Kuwait and neutralizing their military power. Once the Iraqi military was destroyed, it would no longer be necessary to keep a sizable American presence in the region at all. Under these circumstances, the only requirement for a permanent commitment of American forces would be a decision to march on Baghdad and destroy the regime that had brought war in the first place. Such an objective, the administration believed, would lead inescapably to a quagmire from which the United States could not extract itself.

To those made anxious over the amount of damage inflicted on Iraqi frontline conscripts and the collateral damage to civilian installations, the administration argued that the United States had an obligation to its own soldiers and citizens to minimize American casualties to the highest degree possible. The collapse of Iraqi forces came more suddenly than was expected, and invites the retrospective speculation that it might have been achieved through a more graduated or limited application of American power. Yet in all probability the reason for the suddenness of the collapse lay precisely in the adoption of a strategy of overwhelming force. Given the inherent uncertainties of war (and given the prediction of domestic critics that Iraqi ground forces would put up a tenacious defense), it was incumbent on the administration to support the war plan its military advisors had recommended and to break Iraqi resistance as rapidly as possible.

CHAPTER 7

The Motive for the War

The justification the Bush administration offered for its conduct in the gulf war should not necessarily be identified with its motives. A justification for acting, and a motive for doing so, are two different things. One is public, the other private. One appeals to the approbation of mankind, whereas the other normally arises from less disinterested considerations. Justifications and motives may coincide in some respects, but they seldom do so in all. One can be reconstructed on the basis of the public record, whereas the other is necessarily speculative (and will in crucial respects almost certainly remain so even when all the documents are opened for inspection in the distant future). Yet justifications remain of crucial significance, not only because they erect a standard that critics must meet but also because they often shed an important light on motives.

From the beginning of the crisis, the administration took the view that nothing less than an unambiguous humiliation for Saddam Hussein would constitute a policy success in the crisis. If he gained anything from his invasion, his use of force would have succeeded; the administration was determined not only that he should fail but that he should fail spectacularly. In part at least, the motive for this insistence did stem from the strength of the legalist outlook within the American diplomatic tradition, which provided a theory of the causes and remedies for aggressive behavior by criminal states. For all of President Bush's supposed pragmatism, he was a true believer in the theory of aggression that lay at the heart of American legalism. When confronted with Iraq's invasion and annexation of Kuwait, all the elements of that **87** outlook welled up inside him. It touched his deepest beliefs in what America stood for, and recalled what he had fought for as a young man in World War II. There is no reason to question the sincerity of this justification, or to doubt that it formed a crucial motivation for the president.

At the same time, the determination to ensure a spectacular defeat for Saddam Hussein was also due to the vast disparity of power between Iraq and the United States, which prompted the belief that America's status as a superpower rested on the ability to deliver a crushing blow against those who might forcibly challenge its position. "When we win, and we will," as the president said, "we will have taught a dangerous dictator, and any tyrant tempted to follow in his footsteps that the U.S. has a new credibility, and that what we say goes, and that there is no place for lawless aggression in the Persian Gulf and in this new world order that we seek to create. And we mean it." [1] The relative importance of these two considerations—of power and of principle—is difficult to determine, for there was very little in the way of contradiction between them. One appealed to pride, the other to the moral sense. One evoked the image of the most powerful state in the international system, whose writ would be the law of the world; the other the state most committed to considerations of moral principle, whose offended righteousness, once engaged, would not allow even the barest hint of a plea bargain with a criminal state that showed neither remorse nor promise of rehabilitation.

Nor is there reason to doubt that the administration genuinely feared that Iraq might sometime in the future gain possession of nuclear weapons. The striking feature of this particular justification, however, is that it proved too much. If it were true that Saddam Hussein was only six months to a year away from the construction of a single nuclear device, as the administration began insistently claiming in November 1990, and if it were also true that he was immune to the calculations of deterrence, it appeared to follow that war was the only course of action that might ease the danger and deprive him of his incipient nuclear capability. Though administration officials would not acknowl-

88   edge the point, the nuclear peril was not only an argument for speeding up the timetable of Iraq's withdrawal from Kuwait, it was also an argument for waging a preventive war.

More generally, the resolution of the crisis to which the administration was publicly committed—an unconditional withdrawal from Kuwait that would allow Iraq to retain its military capabilities—also, on the administration's own reasoning, entailed very serious defects. When American troops were dispatched to Saudi Arabia in August 1990, the administration informed the Saudis that they would stay only for the duration of the crisis. It told the American people much the same thing. Yet if it was true, as the administration claimed, that its initial deployment of 270,000 troops was necessary for the defense of Saudi Arabia, it would be impossible to fulfill this commitment should Saddam Hussein leave Kuwait with his military power intact. The same dangers presumably attached to a permanent American defensive shield stationed in Saudi Arabia to contain an Iraq that held on to Kuwait would also be attached to the force needed to contain an Iraq that had withdrawn from Kuwait. The only way to resolve this danger was to go to war, thus neutralizing the Iraqi military capabilities that, so long as they were in existence, remained a menace to surrounding nations.

From the outset of the crisis, these considerations had been urged upon the administration by influential voices who said that a war against Iraq was both inevitable and necessary. The advocates of war included editorial boards (*The Wall Street Journal, The New Republic,* and *National Review*), columnists (William Safire, A.M. Rosenthal, Charles Krauthammer, and Jim Hoagland) and former government officials (Henry Kissinger, Richard Perle, and Frank Gaffney). The gravamen of their indictment against sanctions was not that they would fail in getting Saddam Hussein out of Kuwait, which was the main justification the Bush administration urged, but rather that they might succeed disastrously. The basic danger was any settlement that entailed a temporary respite for Iraq while not dealing with the long-range problem represented by its military power. We could either pay now, or pay later (and in far worse circumstances).

Did the president accept this view? The most plausible expla-   **89**
nation, though one that remains speculative, is that he did. On
this view, his decision to double the size of American forces, which
was reached sometime in October 1990, reflected the conclusion
that war was the best way to resolve the crisis. Only a war could
achieve the neutralization of Iraqi military power, and only the
neutralization of Iraqi military power might create the circumstances that would allow the United States to avoid a permanent
commitment of sizable American forces in Saudi Arabia.

At the same time, the political circumstances the president
faced made it impossible to avow this conclusion publicly. Neither
the international coalition the United States had built at the UN
nor domestic opinion at home would readily accept the proposition that a preventive war was necessary to neutralize Iraqi military
capabilities. Though the president declared on more than one
occasion that a war of collective defense for the liberation of
Kuwait might be undertaken without UN approval, just as he later
declared that his authority as commander in chief gave him the
right to go to war without congressional authorization, he clearly
wanted to secure the widest possible support both at home and
abroad for his policy. This he could only do if his avowed aim was
peace. The administration therefore felt itself under a profound
compulsion to portray its buildup of American military forces and
its subsequent ultimatum to Iraq as constituting the best hope for a
peaceful resolution of the crisis.

The likelihood that the administration, as early as October,
saw war as the best resolution of the crisis does not mean that it was
determined to go to war under all circumstances. It was always
possible, though unlikely, that Saddam Hussein would uncondi-
tionally withdraw from Kuwait. Under these circumstances, the
administration could not go to war. In early December, Secretary
Baker made it clear that such a withdrawal would spare Saddam
Hussein the use of American and allied military power against his
country.[2] At the same time, the administration also said that such
a withdrawal would not lead to the lifting of economic sanctions
against him. The United States would offer no guarantees to Iraq if
it agreed to withdraw. "We're not saying get out and all is for-

90   given," as one official put it.[3] Indeed, it seemed highly likely that the United States would agree to the lifting of economic sanctions against Iraq only if Iraq agreed to pay reparations and reduce its military establishment (while also eliminating its weapons of mass destruction). Since the president had suggested, as early as October, that a war crimes trial on the precedent of the Nuremberg Trials following World War II might be appropriate in this instance, it also seemed likely that the United States would agree to lift the sanctions only if Saddam Hussein was removed from power.

Given the character of these demands, it was highly unlikely that Saddam Hussein would accept the offer if he could see any way of retrieving his prestige from this unexpected, though doubtless credible, ultimatum from the American lion. And this, he not unreasonably concluded, he had a fighting chance to do. Virtually from the outset of his occupation of Kuwait, Iraqi forces had been digging in, constructing fortifications, laying minefields, adding reinforcements—all in preparation for the day when American forces would attempt to dislodge them. Though no one could penetrate the inner recesses of his mind, it was unreasonable to think that Saddam Hussein would rate his chances in war as impossibly bad. All his utterances pointed to the conclusion that he believed, as indeed did most American experts, that he would be capable of imposing substantial casualties on American forces. If so, he had at least a fighting chance, not to prevent an American victory over Iraqi forces in Kuwait, but to achieve a serious bloodying of American power.

It was often assumed, after the outbreak of war, that the president had badly misread Saddam Hussein's intentions, and had failed to appreciate that the threat of war could not dislodge him from Kuwait.[4] A more plausible explanation, however, is that the president understood quite clearly the psychological imperatives under which Saddam was operating. Given the disparity between the administration's stated goals (Iraq's unconditional withdrawal from Kuwait) and its unstated aspirations (the destruction of Iraqi military power in war), it found itself in a delicate position. It could not be seen as foreclosing the possibility of a

peaceful settlement; at the same time, it had to surround Saddam **91**
with conditions so onerous as to make his voluntary withdrawal
distinctly unattractive, even as compared with his decisive defeat
in war. The four nos—"No negotiations, no compromises, no
attempts at face saving, and no rewards for aggression"[5]—were
well suited to this purpose. They were a club with which the
administration might assault Saddam's pride and thereby stiffen
his intransigence. Even more effective in this respect was the
vitriolic language the president employed from the first hours of
the crisis. Even if Saddam had been prepared to swallow his pride
in an adroit concession at the last moment, there remained the
administration's determination to maintain economic sanctions
unless other stringent conditions—including Saddam's removal
from power—were also met. On this view, there was no failure of
understanding on the part of the Bush administration; on the
contrary, it read Saddam perfectly, and he duly fell into the trap
the administration had set for him.

The conclusion that the president had war in his heart but
peace on his lips, and that this was certainly true by October, if not
well before, may strike some observers as unduly cynical. As
mendacities in politics go, however, it is not particularly unusual.
In palliation of the lie, if it was a lie, it may be said that the main
opponents of the president's ultimatum in the Congress were
guilty of the same sin. For if it was true that a war for the liberation
of Kuwait risked serious American losses, and if it was true that the
use of force against Iraq might produce unpredictable and chaotic
consequences throughout the Middle East, as the Democratic
opposition believed, then a set of powerful arguments existed
against resorting to war, whether that war was undertaken in
January 1991 or a year later. But it was not the position of the
Democratic leadership opposing President Bush that a war for the
liberation of Kuwait was to be ruled out. Like the president, it too
would not forswear the use of force for this object. In arguing
against the resolution authorizing force, Senate Majority Leader
George Mitchell held that "this is not a debate about whether
force should ever be used. No one proposes to rule out the use of
force. We cannot and should not rule it out."[6]

The congressional debate on the eve of the war thus presented that most interesting of political spectacles—a fraud encountering a deception. The president's fraud was his continual declaration that his own course represented "the last, best hope of peace" when he knew that his aims could only be achieved by a war; the Democrats' deception was in claiming that they disagreed with the president only on the question of timing and that they would at some point be willing to countenance the use of American military force to liberate Kuwait, when their own innermost convictions pointed decisively against war for such an object at any time.

Given the character of this encounter, the president enjoyed substantial advantages over his opponents. Only on constitutional questions did the Democrats hold an unassailable position. It could not be seriously claimed that the president enjoyed the authority to go to war in this instance and for this object without congressional authorization. Such a view was wholly incompatible with the original understanding of the framers of the Constitution and could not be entertained in this instance without nullifying one of the most important provisions of the instrument. At the same time, the president's political position was nearly as unassailable as the Democrat's constitutional position. He had maneuvered the Democrats into the confession that their difference with him was over timing, and this he had the power to resolve.

By committing 500,000 forces to Saudi Arabia, which the Democrats conceded was within his authority as commander in chief, and by delivering, on his own authority, an ultimatum to Saddam, Bush had committed the honor of the American government. Critics might question the wisdom of these measures, bemoan the apparent departure from containment, or arraign the president on a score of lesser points, but it could not be denied that he had committed the United States to a course of action from which the nation could turn away only if it were prepared to incur a severe blow to its prestige. To oppose this step on the basis of the conviction that a war with Iraq for the liberation of Kuwait was not justified—not now, and not ever—would have placed the Democrats on firmer ground, though it might have affected the result **93** only at an earlier stage of the crisis. To oppose war on the deceptive ground that they chose, however, ensured that their position would be afflicted by a fatal handicap and would constitute a barrier the president could easily surmount.

CHAPTER 8

The Case for Punitive Containment

In the end, the crucial questions raised by the war do not rest on the inner motives held by the president but on the public justification for his conduct. However much the president and his advisors may have secretly harbored a desire for waging a preventive war, the war that they were committed to waging was one to liberate Kuwait. Though it may be true that what was presented as the president's dream was in reality his nightmare, and that he feared rather than hoped for an Iraqi withdrawal from Kuwait because it would allow Saddam Hussein to elude his grasp, it was nevertheless the case that if Saddam withdrew from Kuwait the president could not use force against him. In all likelihood, Saddam was convinced that the administration was intent on pursuing him to the bitter end, and hence saw no profit in avoiding the test of arms. In reality, however, the administration would have had no alternative but to stick to the deal it had offered if Saddam decided to surprise the world by an offer that at least approximated the stated American conditions.

Kuwait, then, was crucial. It was Kuwait from which radiated the threats to world order, regional security, and the global economy that the administration repeatedly invoked. It was for Kuwait that time was of the essence, and for Kuwait that sanctions could be shown to promise no immediate result. From the beginning, the president made the immediate restoration of Kuwait's sovereignty a *sine qua non* for the resolution of the crisis. Rhetorically, President Bush always wanted Saddam Hussein out of Kuwait yesterday morning. The status quo was intolerable and had to be changed, through peaceful means if possible, through war if necessary.

Was this commitment necessary? Was it the only feasible   **95**
policy that would have preserved American vital interests and
safeguarded the other values and interests—world order, regional
security, and the global economy—continually invoked by the
administration? It is difficult to believe that it was. An alternative
policy might have been pursued that also promised to secure
American vital interests and was substantially different from the
policy adopted by the administration from the outset of the crisis.

The alternative was a policy of punitive containment.[1] It
would have rested on two central pillars: the extension of a security
guarantee to Saudi Arabia and other gulf states, together with the
determination to maintain economic sanctions against Iraq until
it withdrew from Kuwait and gave satisfactory guarantees of good
behavior in the future. This policy was distinguishable from the
administration's position in ten important respects:

1. In contrast to the administration's decision to dispatch a
270,000-troop armada of soldiers, seamen, airmen, and marines,
an alternative response would have centered the American military commitment to the gulf on land-based airpower, with modest
support from U.S. ground and naval forces. For most of the ground
forces, it would have relied on the contributions of Arab states,
including Saudi Arabia, Egypt, and Syria.

2. In contrast to the administration's willingness to make
the Iraqi occupation of Kuwait a *casus belli*, an alternative response
would have been to forswear the use of American military power
for this object and instead to make the lifting of economic sanctions contingent on Iraq's fulfillment of stringent conditions—
including its withdrawal from Kuwait, its acceptance of the duty to
provide reparations, and its consent to open its nuclear and biological
weapons programs to international inspection. As long as these
conditions were satisfied, the United States might have supported
concessions to Iraq over the two islands—Bubiyan and Warba—that
blocked Iraqi access to the Persian Gulf. In calculating the extent of
reparations owed by Iraq to Kuwait, it might also have taken into
account Iraqi complaints—which may well have been legitimate—
over Kuwaiti drilling practices in the Rumaila oil field.

96   3. Like the administration's policy, punitive containment would not have excluded military reprisals in the event of a further Iraqi military challenge, though one that fell short of an invasion of Saudi Arabia. At the same time, it would have aimed economic sanctions preeminently at Saddam's financial base; over time, it would have been willing to allow limited oil sales by Iraq to mitigate the possibility of a famine or a widespread health crisis among the Iraqi civilian population.

4. In contrast to the administration's policy, punitive containment would not have made Saddam Hussein's removal from power a condition of an acceptable settlement (a condition that only emerged as an explicit goal of administration policy after the war but which was intimated in the president's suggestion of a war crimes tribunal, as well as in other utterances, as early as October 1990).

5. In contrast to the administration's policy, which found the prospect of any protracted standoff with Iraq unacceptable, the alternative response would have taken satisfaction in doing without Iraqi and Kuwaiti oil indefinitely, thereby depriving Iraq of the principal support of its power. It would have placed no timetable on Iraq's withdrawal. It would have said, as the president did in Helsinki, that "If the nations of the world acting together continue, as they have been, to isolate Iraq and deny Saddam the fruits of aggression, we will set in place the cornerstone of an international order more peaceful, stable and secure than any that we have known."[2] But it would have meant it.

6. In contrast to the president, who personalized the quarrel from the very outset, who used every opportunity to denounce Saddam Hussein in vitriolic and heated tones, and who generally treated his adversary in a way calculated to assault his pride and make war inevitable, an alternative policy would have entailed a more measured diplomatic tone that, without retreating from America's stated aims, would nevertheless have encouraged a peaceful resolution of the dispute.

7. A policy of punitive containment would have rested American policy toward Israel on the proposition that Israel's security against the threat posed by Iraq was its own responsibility.

This implied not only that the United States would not have **97**
sought to force Israel to pledge that it would refrain from responding to an Iraqi attack (as the administration did, though in a
different context), but also that we would not have attempted to
prevent Israel from launching air strikes against strategic targets in
Iraq if Israel considered such strikes vital to its security. It is
doubtful, to be sure, that Israel would have launched such an
attack even without U.S. opposition. Still, the logic of staying
Israel's hand carried with it the implication that we would do what
we enjoined the Israelis from doing. An alternative policy would
have rejected this logic.

8. Like the administration's policy, this policy would not
have permitted Saddam Hussein to link Kuwait and Palestine;
unlike the administration, however, the policy of punitive containment would not have used the Iraqi crisis to pry open the door
to a settlement of the Arab-Israeli conflict.

9. Like the president's policy, this alternative would have
appealed to international law in justifying its course of action; but
unlike the president, it would not have elevated the principle
proscribing aggression (which the administration interpreted as
requiring an immediate restoration of the emir's government) to a
position where it overshadowed and indeed eclipsed other important principles of international society, the most relevant of which
in this context is the desirability of minimizing the occasions on
which states do violence to one another.

10. Like the president's policy, punitive containment would
have sought the widest possible consensus in international society
for its course of action; at the same time, it would have made clear
(as the president did, though for different objects) that the United
States had the authority to go to the military aid of threatened
states in the gulf through purely bilateral understandings. Once
the economic embargo was imposed and authority to undertake a
naval and (and later, air) blockade was granted by the Security
Council, it would have made the most of its ability to veto any
proposed settlement not satisfying the conditions that international society, acting in its own defense, had a right to impose.

98   The advantages and disadvantages of these two alternatives
may be considered under two broad headings. One is whether it
was possible to construct a policy of punitive containment that
would have protected the main values and interests invoked by the
administration—world order, regional security, and the global
economy—without incurring onerous burdens or risks for the
United States or other states which we had an interest in protecting. The second is whether such a policy could be maintained over
time, or would rather, by virtue of the freedom of action it gave
Saddam Hussein, lead the sanctions to be abandoned, the diplomatic coalition to collapse, or the protective shield to be withdrawn. The first question reduces itself to whether a policy of
punitive containment held out the promise of vindicating all
American objectives of material and permanent importance; the
second to whether such a policy could be sustained over time.

★ ★ ★

In considering whether the United States ought to have made the
immediate restoration of Kuwaiti sovereignty its principal goal in
the crisis, it is useful to remember that the United States had no
formal or even informal obligation to do so on August 2, 1990.
Relations between the United States and Kuwait since the first oil
crisis in 1973 had been normally cool and sometimes hostile. In
keeping with its policy of appeasing its large Palestinian diaspora,
Kuwait had embraced positions at the United Nations that put it
on a par with America's most inveterate adversaries.[3] No "mutual
security treaty," the name used for arrangements in which the
United States agrees to supply protection to another state, and the
other state agrees to be protected, existed between the two states.
Nor was there an "executive understanding" to that effect between
the Kuwaiti government and the Bush administration or any of its
predecessors. The only formal arrangement between the two states
was the reflagging of a limited number of Kuwaiti oil tankers
during the closing stages of the war between Iran and Iraq, an
action that entitled such vessels, by virtue of their newly acquired
American nationality, to protection by the U.S. Navy. But this
agreement fell well short of—and indeed was entirely distinct
from—a security relationship between the two states. No such

agreement existed. Indeed, none was even requested by the   **99**
Kuwaitis until the Iraqi invasion was upon them.

A particular obligation to come to Kuwait's aid, then, formed
no part of the historic relationship between the two states. Nor did
such an obligation exist by virtue of general American commitments to the protection of free nations. Kuwait was not a democratic state. Representative institutions had enjoyed a limited role
in Kuwait since the 1960s, but its assembly had been dissolved by
the emir in 1986. The great wealth that oil had brought allowed
the monarchy to maintain a welfare state of considerable liberality
for subjects of the emir. In a region where autocratic police states
were the norm, it had a more open political system than most; in
an area marked by widespread poverty, it maintained a far higher
standard of material comfort. But it remained, in essential respects, an absolute monarchy. However much liberty was taken in
defining membership within "the free world," it could not be said
with candor that Kuwait formed a part of it. *

Nor, finally, was there an obligation to Kuwait by virtue of
the commitments the United States made on entering the United
Nations in 1945. The charter contained no generalized commitment to the "territorial integrity and political independence" of
existing states, such as the League of Nations had undertaken to
uphold. Indeed, such a commitment was purposely excluded by
the framers of the UN Charter, who substituted instead a more
ambiguous commitment to "international peace and security"
(Article I) and gave the Security Council absolute discretion in
determining how such threats were to be addressed.

---

* The record of the Kuwaiti government since the liberation underscores these
considerations. Its determination to expel virtually all of the 400,000 Palestinians who had lived in Kuwait before the war, including families who had
resided there for several generations, was an exceptionally cruel act. While
technically not in violation of international law, which provides governments
with virtually unlimited discretion over resident aliens, it underscored the
degree to which the Kuwaiti government felt itself at liberty to ignore standards of individual accountability commonly recognized in the West. On the
record of the Kuwaiti government after the war, see A *Victory Turned Sour:
Human Rights in Kuwait Since Liberation* (New York: Middle East Watch,
1991).

100   If there were obligations to seek an immediate restoration of the emir's government, they arose not from considerations of good faith but rather of humanity. There was little question that Iraq's conquest of Kuwait entailed great brutality. Iraq systematically looted Kuwait of its movable wealth from the first moments of the invasion; it employed torture on a considerable scale, and it took harsh reprisals against the Kuwaiti resistance that sprang up after the invasion. More generally, the occupation created a climate of fear among the conquered population that entailed widespread psychological anguish.

It may be acknowledged that the brutality of Iraq's occupation made it desirable, on humanitarian grounds, to reverse it as soon as possible. Whether it formed a compelling justification to do so, however, must be assessed against the human costs of using force on a massive scale to effect the restoration of Kuwait. The suffering such a use of force inflicted also fell widely on innocents. Despite the Bush administration's insistence (by its actions though not its words) on applying to Iraq a doctrine of collective responsibility, it would be difficult to make out the claim that Iraq's men, women, and children bore general responsibility for the sins of their rulers. If general considerations of humanity are established as a criterion in determining the justification for U.S. policy, they fail to establish in this instance an obligation to seek the immediate restoration of Kuwait through war. The suffering to innocents brought by war, at least in quantitative terms, appears to have been substantially in excess of the suffering relieved.[4]

These considerations do not establish that the Bush administration was wrong in making the restoration of the emir's government an objective of American diplomacy in the crisis. Whatever the defects of the Kuwaiti royal family, it did enjoy good title in international law over its territorial domain, and it was important to stipulate that the restoration of the emir's government would be a necessary (though not sufficient) condition for lifting the oil embargo against Iraq. At the same time, the United States had no particular or general obligation to the Kuwaiti royal family to seek an immediate restoration of its rule. Insofar as the American government felt the tug of humanitarian considerations in contemplating the brutalities of the Iraqi occupation, it was also

obligated to consider the likely human consequences of the deci- **101**
sion to use force on the scale that it did. These consequences
pointed away from war as a morally preferable way of resolving the
crisis.

One of the principal claims of the Bush administration—that
sanctions could not promise to effect an immediate restoration of
Kuwaiti sovereignty—was thus perfectly true, but its evident implication was not. It was true that sanctions promised no immediate result. It was not true that the United States had an obligation,
either to itself or to others, to effect an immediate result. Insofar as
there was such an obligation, it rested on humanitarian considerations that were outweighed by the likely calamities of a war.

★   ★   ★

In opposition to these considerations, it may be argued that
Saddam's continued possession of Kuwait in itself constituted a
victory and would set a bad example. The longer he stayed, and the
longer he defied the international coalition arrayed against him,
the more it would be said that he had profited from his conquest.
This contention, however, was plainly at odds with the draconian
economic sanctions imposed on Iraq immediately following its
invasion. Those sanctions were almost completely successful in
stopping Iraqi oil exports, and Iraqi imports were reduced by 90
percent. Iraq's GNP fell almost immediately by 40 percent. In
their severity, these economic sanctions were unprecedented in
modern history.[5]

The effectiveness of the sanctions was made possible by the
peculiar circumstances that existed in the Persian Gulf, where the
wealth of states was due almost entirely to their exports of oil.
Such exports constituted the lifeblood of the Iraqi regime. Revenues from oil exports constituted virtually the whole of Iraq's
foreign exchange earnings. The vast edifice of military and civilian projects that the Baathist party had pursued for twenty years
was reared on this foundation. It had fueled ambitious schemes of
social and economic development; it had made Iraq an attractive
place to do business for foreign governments and private arms
smugglers; it had enabled Iraq, during the war with Iran, to

102   minimize the privations to the civilian population that normally accompany a long and bitter struggle with a foreign adversary. A protracted embargo on Iraqi oil exports would place these achievements in grave jeopardy. Saddam Hussein's alarm over the magnitude of the financial crisis facing Iraq had been one of his principal motives for invading Kuwait. To have been denied indefinitely not only the fruits of his aggression against Kuwait but also virtually all proceeds from Iraq's own oil exports (save for the trickle that might escape on trucks through Jordan) would have constituted a relentless and even staggering blow to his power base.

Worse from Iraq's point of view was that such an embargo could be maintained indefinitely with little damage to Western interests. Excess capacity in the world oil market was such that the loss of exports from Iraq and Kuwait (around 4.5 million barrels a day) could be and was made up entirely by expanded production elsewhere, preeminently from Saudi Arabia. Though near-term contracts in the oil futures market rose quickly and reached nearly $40 a barrel by late September 1990, a great part of the increase was due to war fears rather than the existence of a long-term gap between expected production and consumption. (Throughout the crisis, near-term contracts, reversing the normal pattern, were far higher than contracts in the more distant future). By October it was clear that the lost Iraqi and Kuwaiti production had been entirely made up. Had the Bush administration, at the outset of the crisis, pushed onto the market one to two million barrels a day from U.S. strategic petroleum reserves, and had it declared, as General Schwarzkopf did in October, that Iraq did not enjoy the capability through aerial assault of shutting down oil producing or exporting capacity in neighboring states, even the short-term disruptions might have been greatly mitigated.

The existence of spare production capacity to make up for the loss of Iraq's embargoed oil was a strategic factor of prime importance. It reversed the situation that had prevailed in the late 1970s, when Western embargoes on producer exports (for instance, against Iran for having seized the hostages) were scarcely considered as a tool of Western policy because of the grievous self-inflicted injury they would have entailed in the form of exploding oil prices. In both 1980 and 1990, a condition of asymmetrical **103** interdependence prevailed, but owing to the emergence of the production overhang, which persisted throughout the 1980s, the relative economic power of producers and consumers had changed drastically. In 1980, the asymmetries favored America's adversaries; in 1990, they favored us.

Under these circumstances, it strained credulity to assert that Saddam Hussein had turned a profit on the operation. In truth, he was like a man who plotted a clever bank robbery and who succeeded so far as to lay his hands on the gold within the vault, only later to discover that he was locked inside and incapable of making use of the riches at his fingertips. By the theft, he had seized enough of the necessities of life to sustain him through a long ordeal. He had taken hostages. But the great prize he had sought was denied him. Though bold and intrepid, his plan had miscarried. With each passing month he could look forward to greater and greater privations. Under these circumstances, it took a hyperbolic imagination to think that the world would envy him for his position, or seek to emulate his example.

The administration's continued appeal to world order was odd for other reasons as well. Though the principle that aggression should not pay is an important one, the degree to which it is important rests partly on the circumstances in which the infraction occurs. When President Bush compared Saddam to Hitler, and the post–cold war world with a relapse to the anarchy of the 1930s if Saddam did not leave Kuwait, he ignored the salient differences between that epoch and our own. The Axis powers represented a formidable concentration of power, whereas by comparison Iraq's was minuscule; the Axis states, up until 1941, excelled at the strategy of *divide et impera*, whereas Iraq had the whole world in league against it; the material, technological, and human resources of the Axis states were broad and deep, whereas Iraq's power base rested exclusively on oil, of which it was now deprived, and terror, which could only carry it so far.

It was not only the sheer disparity of power between the Axis and Iraq that made the comparison with the 1930s absurd; also relevant in this regard was that the major goal of states in the

104   contemporary world was material advancement rather than territorial aggrandizement. When the president sent out his warning
to potential despots and dictators around the world, it was reasonable to ask precisely which states he was talking about. In fact,
there were virtually none that presented the threat that Iraq held
out to Kuwait. To expect a general upsurge of aggressive behavior
among states in the absence of an immediate restoration of
Kuwaiti sovereignty was unreasonable not only because few states
had the criminal disposition of Iraq, but also because few states
presented, as Kuwait certainly did, such an inviting target.

The threat posed by Iraq was not only fundamentally different from that posed by the Axis powers in the 1930s, it was also
entirely distinct from the danger posed by the communist bloc in
the post–World War II era, a danger that had led the United
States to abandon its historic policy of noninvolvement in the
political affairs of other nations. Though there were certainly
instances in which the threats to American prestige, and the
firmness with which we would maintain our commitments, were
exaggerated, it must be remembered that behind each regional
challenge to order that occurred during the cold war lay the global
threat to order posed by the Soviet Union. It was not unreasonable
to find a connection between the successful aggression of a North
Korea or a North Vietnam and the encouragement which might
thereby be given the Soviet Union. But in back of Iraq there stood
only the will of Saddam Hussein.

★   ★   ★

Insofar as Iraq posed a threat to world order, then, it did so by
virtue of the threats it posed to regional security and the global
economy. Had nothing been done to contain Iraq, American
interests in regional security and the global economy would in all
likelihood have been seriously threatened. Saudi Arabia alone sat
on top of an estimated 20 percent of the world's oil reserves; with
his conquest and annexation of Kuwait, Saddam Hussein had
added another 10 percent of world reserves to the 10 percent he
already controlled. To have left the Saudis to their own devices
would have carried the serious risk that oil production and pricing
decisions would for the indefinite future be greatly influenced by a

regime whose hostility to the West could be taken for granted. In **105** conjuring the dangers that such a situation would have entailed, it was difficult to know which would be worse: a revival of the oil weapon that might drive prices through the roof and wreak havoc on the world economy, or the maintenance of trading arrangements with Iraq that would allow Saddam Hussein to greatly enhance his war chest. Unless Iraqi power was contained and Saudi Arabia was protected, it was not implausible to think that both specters might eventually have to be faced.

The containment of further Iraqi aggression against Saudi Arabia and other gulf states, then, was a vital American interest. It was something for which Americans might sacrifice their own blood and shed the blood of others. But the military protection of Saudi Arabia was not an inordinately difficult undertaking. Saudi Arabia, unlike Kuwait, enjoyed long-standing though unpublicized contacts with the United States military. The facilities for the rapid projection of airpower into Saudi Arabia had been built up in the 1980s as part of a U.S.–Saudi agreement achieved by the Reagan administration in 1981. Not only could Saudi Arabia's military protection be secured; it could be secured rapidly.

Had the military protection of Saudi Arabia been the aim of the Bush administration, a force based primarily on U.S. airpower, together with ground forces provided by regional states, would have sufficed to ensure an effective defense of Saudi Arabia. Iraq's forces were a potent match for any army of the region, but it had crucial weaknesses against the U.S. Air Force. Iraq's air defense systems were primitive and easily foiled. Under these circumstances, the United States rapidly acquired the capability to deny Iraqi forces either tactical or strategic mobility. It might be said that the significance of this overwhelming aerial superiority was not grasped until the war proved it to be the case, but this is to misread the nature of the debate that occurred over airpower before the war. This debate was not focused on the ability of U.S. airpower to decimate an advancing armored force that had no aircover—virtually all experts held that it could—but rather on the capacity of airpower to destroy forces that had constructed extensive fortifications in preparation for the day of attack. Those

106   who foresaw that such an attack on fortified positions would totally break Iraqi resistance and make the imminent ground war one in which virtually no hostile fire was encountered may justly claim prescience in military science. At the same time, the unexpected success of airpower in the offensive (and intrinsically more difficult) role assigned to it underlines the ease with which it might have performed a defensive role. A defensive shield, it was evident both at the time and subsequently, was readily obtainable and was in fact achieved early on in the crisis.

It seems evident, therefore, that the Bush administration's initial deployment of 270,000 troops was, from the very outset, well in excess of that required for a purely defensive mission. It may safely be concluded that the administration realized this, and that it had not inadvertently set off a deployment that produced unanticipated and unwanted pressures to make offensive war. Though President Bush declared on August 8, 1990, in a prepared statement, that the deployment (whose total numbers were shrouded in secrecy but which was reported at the time to be around 200,000) was "wholly defensive," in the exchange with reporters that followed he said only that American forces "were in a defensive mode right now."[6] A week after the deployment announcement, he said that military force would be considered if all else failed to dislodge the Iraqis from Kuwait. If it is true, as seems evident, that the president was not entirely candid in declaring the mission of the force to be wholly defensive, it might be said on his behalf that there was no reason to advertise the offensive option at a time when the defensive deployment was just beginning. Besides, within the first week of the crisis, several administration officials had made it known in unattributed remarks to journalists that the possibility of war "was in the background"[7] even when they refused to go on record as threatening it.

Whatever the assumptions that guided civilian and military officials in their decision to send a force of 270,000 troops to Saudi Arabia, it seems apparent that had a purely defensive force been desired it could have been improvised, despite the absence of any alternatives in the military's only deployment plan (the so-called Plan 90 1002). In fact, when Secretary Cheney and General

Schwarzkopf visited Saudi Arabia to offer a large scale commit- **107**
ment, the Saudis had been taken aback at the size of the force
being offered. King Fahd had expected airpower alone. His attitude was significant, because it showed that the Saudis would have
been satisfied (and felt themselves secure) with the commitment
of U.S. airpower. It also shows that an American offensive against
Iraq over Kuwait was not a condition of Saudi Arabia's decision to
accept American forces. *

★   ★   ★

One drawback of a policy of punitive containment was that it
could promise no immediate relief for the hostages Iraq had seized
in the first weeks of the crisis. This does not show, however, that
the alternative course the president pursued was a wise one under
the circumstances. In the event, it turned out the American
threat of force against Iraq led Saddam to release the hostages in
early December. His motives in taking this step seem clear
enough; he believed that it would make it more difficult for the

---

* One of the ironies of civil-military decision making during the crisis is that
U.S. military leaders, who tended to favor containment, recommended an
initial deployment of forces that was inconsistent with containment. In their
desire to build up an overwhelming force that would foreclose any thoughts
Saddam Hussein might have entertained of further aggression to the south,
they succeeded in creating a force that undermined containment as a long-
term strategy. Such, at least, appears to have been the case with the Chairman
of the Joint Chiefs of Staff, Colin Powell. See the account in Bob Woodward
(*The Commanders*, New York: Simon & Schuster, 1991). Still more ironically,
there is much evidence to suggest that civilian policymakers believed that the
initial force of 270,000 would be sufficient for an offensive option and were
surprised to learn in October that the military considered a doubling of the
force necessary to produce such a capability. (See Elizabeth Drew, "Letter
from Washington," *The New Yorker*, December 3, 1990.)
   This civilian expectation is significant. Because of it, an explanation of the
announced move to an offensive option in November which stresses the pressures
for war created by the initial deployment seems misplaced. Here, as in 1914, the
dominant factor pushing the antagonists toward war was not the pressures exerted
by the military deployments themselves but the political ambitions of civilian
leaders. Civilians may have been trapped by the logic of the initial deployment to
Saudi Arabia; if so, however, it was a trap largely of their own devising. Indeed,
from the outset the administration believed that the more traps it constructed for
the United States the more credible would be its threats against Saddam.

108   United States to go to war. In fact, however, it made it much easier
for the United States to go to war, as President Bush remarked
immediately (and before most of the hostages had been released).

Before the release of the hostages, the United States had
announced the doubling of American forces; it had secured UN
authorization for war; it had set a deadline. It may safely be
assumed that when the administration did these things, which
amounted to a conditional decision to go to war, it had no
expectation that the hostages would be freed before the outbreak
of hostilities. There is no evidence that the administration anticipated that Saddam would miscalculate so badly as to surrender his
primary shield against a U.S.–led air assault on Iraq's strategic
installations.

When the administration made its conditional decision to go
to war, Iraq still held approximately 2,000 Western hostages. Of
these, somewhat less than half were American citizens. As many
as 100 Americans had been moved to the most likely targets of an
American air attack on Iraq. From the first hours of the crisis, the
president said that the fate of the hostages, though of great
concern to him, would not affect American policy. He also promised the American people that if the United States went to war, it
would not undertake hostilities with one hand tied behind its back
(as it presumably had done in Vietnam). Force, if necessary, would
be used "suddenly, massively, and decisively." Civilians would not
interfere in matters (for instance, the selection of targets) that
were in the province of military decision making, as the Johnson
administration had repeatedly done in Vietnam. At the same
time, military officials made it clear in briefings to administration
officials that attacks on Iraqi command, control, and communication facilities, its air force and air defense systems, and its chemical, biological, and nuclear weapons facilities, would constitute
the first, and indispensable, phase of an American offensive.

Had Saddam not released the hostages, and had he placed an
even greater number at strategic installations in preparation for
the day of attack, would the administration have altered American
war plans? To have done so would have meant abandoning many of
its prior pledges. Not to have done so would have meant directly

sacrificing the lives of the hostages, many of whom were not **109**
American citizens. No one knows how the administration would
have resolved this dilemma; each alternative would have involved
great risks. The first course of action would have meant the
sacrifice of one of its principal military objectives (the destruction
of Iraq's ABC facilities); it would have meant sparing targets
whose destruction the military claimed was indispensable if the
American offensive in Kuwait were to succeed at the lowest possible cost in the lives of American soldiers; it would have advertised
to the world that the taking of hostages could affect American
policy, and dramatically so; and it would have probably required
detailed civilian review of targeting plans.

These prospects could not have appeared as anything but
deeply unattractive to the administration; the alternative, however, would have been equally unattractive. Any military action
that sacrificed the lives of the hostages under Iraq's control, even
in a righteous cause, would have had unpredictable repercussions
on American public opinion. It might have gravely complicated
American relations with foreign governments whose nationals lost
their lives in an American-led aerial assault. However much the
administration might plead that Saddam had no right under international law to use hostages as shields and thus bore direct responsibility for their deaths, there was no guarantee that such a case
would have been persuasive in the court of public opinion,
whether at home or abroad. The fact would have remained that
the immediate agent of their demise was the American-led aerial
assault on Iraq.

That the administration did not have to face this dilemma
was a case of pure luck, an unexpected gift from a man not known
for such kindnesses. Saddam came bitterly to regret releasing the
hostages; from his point of view, it was indeed a great error. It
made sense only if he were prepared to make further concessions,
but such concessions as he might subsequently have made depended on a positive response from Washington. Not only was a
positive response not forthcoming, the release of the hostages
seemed if anything to harden the American position. The administration's course of action, on the other hand, was fraught with

110   extraordinary risk; it represented the voluntary courting of a dilemma from which there would have been no easy escape. The distinct possibility remains that President Bush, despite his concern for the hostages, had embarked in October on a course of action that would have ultimately required their sacrifice.

CHAPTER 9

Proliferation and Preventive War

The most insistent claim that a policy of punitive containment would not give sufficient protection against further Iraqi aggression arose from the specter that Iraq might acquire weapons of mass destruction. Most of the leading advocates of war left no doubt that, if the choice had to be made, an outcome that deprived Iraq of its weapons of mass destruction but not Kuwait would be far superior to an outcome in which Iraq's atomic, biological, and chemical (ABC) capabilities were retained but Kuwait was given up.

Though Iraq's nonconventional weapons capabilities were often linked together during the confrontation, its chemical, biological, and nuclear weapons programs were at different stages of development and posed sharply different threats. Its chemical weapons programs were the most advanced, but the least worrisome. Indeed, the operational obstacles that Iraq faced were such that its chemical weapons arsenal did not qualify as a weapon of mass destruction.[1] About its biological weapons programs, hardly anything was known, but there was little evidence to suggest that Iraq had overcome the severe obstacles that made such weapons dangerous to handle and operationally unreliable.

Iraq's program to develop nuclear weapons raised the most crucial question. The debate over this question before the war took place in an atmosphere of profound uncertainty, for little was known about the status of Iraq's program. Expert opinion was sharply divided over the progress Iraq had made in developing nuclear weapons. Some took the view that Iraq was anywhere

112   between five and ten years away from developing nuclear weapons, a timetable that might itself be impossible to reach because of the economic sanctions imposed upon it. Others, including the Bush administration, argued that such a capability might be much closer than was generally expected. The prewar dispute centered mainly on whether Iraq would be capable of diverting to illicit uses the fuel salvaged from its Osiraq reactor, destroyed by Israeli warplanes in 1981. Given sufficiently ingenious engineering, such material might have been sufficient to produce a single truck-bound nuclear device with the explosive power of the Nagasaki bomb. American intelligence estimated that, with the skills of American weapons designers, Iraq might be able to construct a primitive nuclear device "within six months to a year, and probably longer."[2]

In the aftermath of the war, it was discovered that Iraq was much further along in its nuclear development program than had been generally thought, confirming the Bush administration's fears, though for reasons unrelated to its original suspicions. Using a process for producing highly enriched uranium that had been developed during America's development of atomic weapons in the 1940s, Iraq had developed in secret, and outside the safeguards of the International Atomic Energy Commission, the capability of producing "at least one bomb's worth of high-enriched uranium annually"[3] once its programs were fully operational—a capability that experts said might have been reached by late 1992. Questions continue to surround Iraq's ability to convert this fissile material into warheads or bombs; at the least, however, Iraq was further along in overcoming the obstacles to a nuclear capability than had previously been thought.

For those who had advocated war in the first place, and for many who had not, these revelations confirmed that a policy of punitive containment would have failed and might well have led to disaster. On this view, it would have been very difficult, if not impossible, to deter Saddam Hussein from the use of such weapons once he acquired them. Not only did Iraq's incipient nuclear capabilities justify a preventive war against it, they also provided an object lesson in how to deal with future nuclear threats.

Normally discordant voices all along the political spectrum approved the use of force to prevent nuclear proliferation by states deemed aggressive and expansionist, if peaceful measures failed to secure this objective.[4] The advent of precision-guided munitions, together with the passing of the cold war, provides the opportunity for such a policy; a lost faith in deterrence provides the motive.

Whether this sweeping conclusion is justified by the gulf crisis is open to serious question. It should be remembered that the same temptation arose during the cold war when first the Soviet Union and then China developed nuclear weapons. It was said in the early 1950s about the Soviet Union, just as it was later said in the early to mid-1960s about China, that it would be impossible to enter into a deterrent relationship with either regime, and that once either power acquired the capability of striking the United States with nuclear weapons our ability to contain their expansion would be fatally undermined. When the desirability of preventive war was raised in conjunction with those fears, however, the administrations of the day rejected it as being not only imprudent but also immoral and wrong. That viewpoint now seems to be a thing of the past. Given the absence of a great power adversary, prudence apparently need no longer restrain the United States to the extent it once did. Since moral and legal restraints are not unaffected by prudential considerations, they, too, appear to have a declining relevance. There is a distinct possibility that, had Americans reasoned about the perils of nuclear proliferation then as they seem to be reasoning about them now, and had the United States possessed the highly accurate weapons then that it possesses now, the "long peace" associated with the cold war would have been considerably shorter than it was.

The great danger of a policy of preventive war is that, in seeking to ward off threats to the future security of a state, it entertains aspirations that can only be satisfied by frequent war. That is the central reason why, in the twentieth-century movement to restrict the occasions on which states may lawfully resort to force, preventive war has been generally condemned. Heretofore, the United States has been a consistent supporter of this movement. From the vantage point of its hegemonial military

114   position, however, it now finds itself tempted to dispense with this
rule when it proves inconvenient.

It can be argued that Saddam Hussein's Iraq, by virtue of its
odious characteristics, represented an exception to the rule against
preventive war, and while in normal circumstances the United
States should attempt to restrict nuclear proliferation through
measures short of war, in this case there were good reasons for
acting militarily to prevent Iraq's acquisition of a nuclear capability. On this view, there was a serious question whether it was
possible to deter Saddam Hussein, to close off certain avenues of
escape from his predicament by making those escape routes appear
altogether too risky. Though this question was linked closely to
the nuclear danger, it was also relevant to the broader question of
how the crisis might play out and how Saddam might respond,
even without access to weapons of mass destruction, to the impressive array of forces ranged against him.

The Bush administration's ostensible attitude to this question
was curious. It professed to believe that Saddam would respond to
compellance, but argued at the same time that he would not
observe the restraints of deterrence. The threat of war could make
him get out of Kuwait, but it could not prevent him from using his
military power for further adventures. What made this peculiar
was that compellance has normally, and for obvious reasons, been
considered a more difficult undertaking than deterrence. It rests
on the change, rather than the preservation, of the status quo. It
requires movement rather than *stasis*. Between the administration's declarations that containment was unstable and its affirma-
tions that the threat of war would force Saddam from Kuwait, it
showed a striking inconsistency, at least if seen through the prism
of this seldom incontroverted theorem of political physics.[5]

The war demonstrated that Saddam would not respond to
threats of compellance, particularly when such threats appeared
to him to require his political suicide. It did not show, however,
that he would not respond to the calculations of deterrence. In
fact, his actions during the five and a half month crisis reflected a
certain circumspection. He gave orders to avoid an armed confrontation with American naval vessels. He ordered no spectacu-

lar acts of terrorism (though he may not have enjoyed the power to **115**
do so). After first sealing off the foreign embassies in Kuwait that
refused to recognize the legitimacy of his new acquisition, he later
sent provisions to the holdouts. He released the hostages. His
motives in so acting were to avoid giving the United States a
provocation for the use of force against him.

Nor does Saddam's initial invasion of Kuwait show that he
could not have been deterred from further crossing the various red
lines that American diplomacy might have set before him. No real
attempt to deter him had previously been made. In his conversa-
tions on the eve of the invasion with the American ambassador to
Iraq, April Glaspie, he had been told that the United States "had
no opinion on the Arab-Arab conflicts, like your border disagreement with Kuwait."[6] In making this declaration, which was
perfectly consistent with the prevailing U.S. policy toward Iraq,
the ambassador did not give Saddam a green light to invade and
occupy Kuwait, as many critics later charged. Rather, she gave
him a green light to resolve his dispute with Kuwait over the
Rumaila oil field and the contested islands of Bubiyan and Warbah
that blocked Iraq's access to the Persian Gulf. Because the United
States seems not to have anticipated that Iraq would seize the
whole and not a part, the warnings that were issued were vague or
nonexistent. The firmest statement was issued by State Department spokeswoman Margaret Tutwiler on July 24, 1990, who
stated that the United States "remain[s] strongly committed to
supporting the individual and collective self-defense of our friends
in the gulf, with whom we have deep and long-standing ties." This
statement, however, was preceded by the observation that "we do
not have any defense treaties with Kuwait and there are no special
defense or security commitments to Kuwait."[7] The United States
gave Saddam Hussein no green light to undertake the invasion and
annexation of Kuwait, but it gave him no red light either. *

---

* The transcript of the July 25, 1990, conversation between Ambassador Glaspie
and Saddam Hussein was released by Iraq on September 11, 1990. Immediately after the release of the transcript, administration officials privately
confirmed that it was "essentially accurate." Pleading its privilege of confiden-

116   Whatever conclusions Saddam Hussein drew from these statements, it seems evident that, in undertaking his invasion, he did not anticipate the response that he received. He probably discounted the possibility that Saudi Arabia would admit American forces or that draconian economic sanctions would be imposed against him. Under those anticipated circumstances, he no doubt thought he could weather the strident though impotent condemnations sure to issue from world capitals. His calculations went awry, and he found himself in a thoroughgoing and inescapable predicament. But he did calculate. The invasion was not the act of a madman. The rich and indolent Kuwaitis appeared to be, and were in fact, a perfect match for his relatively poorer yet rising state.

Nor did Saddam's past conduct, though one of extraordinary brutality, demonstrate the psychological profile of a madman. Though he seems to have taken sadistic pleasure in personally

---

tial communications, it refused to release the ambassador's summary of the meeting. Throughout the crisis and the war, the ambassador was placed under a strict rule of public silence by the State Department. In the aftermath of the war, however, the two congressional committees on foreign affairs requested her appearance before them. The supposed July 25 transcript, she then declared, was largely fabricated by the Iraqis. It was a piece of disinformation. Not only had Saddam Hussein been warned, he had been warned sternly. "I told him orally we would defend our vital interests, we would support our friends in the Gulf, we would defend their sovereignty and integrity." (See Thomas L. Friedman, "Envoy to Iraq, Faulted in Crisis, Says She Warned Hussein Sternly," *The New York Times*, March 21, 1991.) When asked why the Iraqi transcript was not immediately denounced, and why the administration had waited so long to set the record straight, Ambassador Glaspie explained that "The administration wanted to work on its job of collecting a coalition and winning the war." It was not a time, she said, for retrospectives.

This explanation persuaded no one. Hawks and doves united in finding the proffered excuse incredible. Had the facts been as Ambassador Glaspie represented them to be in March 1991, the administration had no conceivable motive to disguise the fact in September 1990. Yet, on its own account, it had done so. The international coalition would have been strengthened, and not weakened, by the knowledge that Iraq had not only invaded a defenseless country but had done so in defiance of clear and explicit warnings by the United States. The only plausible explanation is that there were no such warnings.

dispatching his adversaries, he does not appear to have killed randomly. If you kept your eyes closed and your mouth shut, it was possible to remain safe, even in the Republic of Fear. Only if you questioned the absolute obedience owed to the great leader, or were in a position to challenge his rule (by acquiring, for instance, an independent base of power in the army) did you risk your head. When he used chemical weapons on the Iranians, he did so at a time when he rightly believed that the world, fearing an Iranian victory, would publicly condemn but secretly applaud the act. When he gassed the Kurds, he believed, and believed rightly, that he could do so with relative impunity. The record showed that he would employ any measure, however odious, and employ any weapon, however destructive, if he thought that he would profit by it. It does not show a similar proclivity to take such actions if the price would be a certain and devastating retaliation against Iraq.

★   ★   ★

Even if these considerations are deemed persuasive, there remains the threat that an Iraqi nuclear capability would have posed to Israel. This threat was undoubtedly a key concern of those outside critics who urged that the United States embark on a war. The American commitment to Israel's security, it was intimated, could only be vindicated through a preventive strike comparable to that which Israel had launched in 1981 against Iraq, but on a far larger scale, since it was aimed not only at Iraq's atomic, biological, and chemical capabilities but its conventional capabilities as well. There were two problems with making this reasoning the basis of an American war against Iraq.

First, though the United States ought to look with grave concern on threats to Israel's physical security, it is unreasonable to make the attitude of the Israeli government a determining factor in how such threats may best be countered. Though Israelis may have been convinced that Saddam's sheer hatred of Jews was sufficient to overpower his fear of devastating retaliation, such a fear was unreasonable. It provided the United States with no justification to take the kind of action this country had denied itself when faced with the prospect of Soviet and Chinese nuclear

118   proliferation in the earlier years of the cold war. Given Israel's own
sizable nuclear capability, estimated at anywhere from one hundred to two hundred bombs, Iraq had nothing to gain, and everything to lose, from such an attack.

Secondly, there were reasons for doubting whether the long-
term relationship between the United States and Israel would be
well served if the United States greatly increased its responsibility
for the protection of the Jewish state. Traditionally, the strategic
doctrine of Israel has been based on the firm conviction that it
would not rely on others—preeminently, the United States—to
satisfy its security needs. It gladly accepted financial and military
assistance from the United States, and always urged that these
levels of assistance be increased, but in matters of war and peace it
disdained the assistance of others. It would take care of itself. This
doctrine was impaired by the gulf war. If the United States had an
obligation to go to war to protect Israel's security, it seemed to
follow that the United States, having assumed this ostensible
duty, was thereby entitled to a right of judgment concerning the
broader political conditions by which the Arab-Israeli dispute
might be settled. This right, however, was not acknowledged
either by Israel or by its principal supporters in the United States,
both of whom were strongly opposed to drawing this conclusion. *

The conviction that Iraq, even if it succeeded in acquiring a
handful of operationally usable nuclear weapons, could have been
deterred from using them, is not a demonstrable proposition. It

---

* The Bush administration was not on record as acknowledging an obligation to
go to war to protect Israel's security. At the same time, however, it clearly
believed that in going to war it had done Israel a favor for which it was entitled
to gratitude. That it received very little was subsequently viewed with considerable dismay and even provided the occasion for protest on the part of the
administration. In one respect, the administration's claim was not very credible, for the Bush administration clearly went to war for its own reasons, of
which concern for Israel's security was distinctly secondary. Nevertheless, it is
also the case that Israel did pressure the United States to wage a preventive
war, for an object in which it was vitally interested. The conclusion seems
irresistible that, having urged the Americans to war, a war which it deemed
indispensable for its own security, Israel did concede an American role in
providing for Israel's security, and thus in the broader resolution of the Arab-
Israeli conflict, that had not existed before.

rests upon a faith in deterrence that, however well-grounded in **119** reason and in the experience of the nuclear age, is nevertheless unprovable. It is the case, moreover, that so long as American policy was predicated on the offensive use of force to drive Iraq from Kuwait, the nuclear specter did justify a shorter rather than a longer timetable. Nuclear weapons, however primitive, would have given Saddam Hussein a greater measure of protection against an American offensive. The policy of punitive contain-ment, however, rested on the maintenance of a militarily defen-sive posture; on its behalf, all that need be claimed is that such a posture would have succeeded in containing and deterring Sad-dam. The uncertainties surrounding Iraq's nuclear posture were sufficiently great to justify making the lifting of sanctions contin-gent on Iraq's renunciation of weapons of mass destruction. These uncertainties also justified a program to develop defenses capable of dealing with the nuclear threats posed by small to medium powers. But it is a highly problematic, indeed dangerous, step from such measures of precaution to a strategic doctrine that justifies preventive war.

CHAPTER 10

Time as an Enemy

Even on their own terms, the military, economic, and diplomatic forces that a policy of punitive containment could array against Iraq were quite striking. More extraordinary was the contrast they afforded with the constellation of forces that had prevailed during more than a decade of confrontation between the United States and adversarial regimes in the gulf. In the past, the ability of the United States to place forces of any kind in the gulf, by virtue of the domestic constraints under which all Arab regimes labored, seemed highly questionable; in 1990, Saudi reservations evaporated, and they declared themselves willing to accept a powerful American force. In the past, the oil weapon had normally been considered the sole and exclusive property of producer regimes; in 1990, it was a weapon that might be wielded by consumers. In the past, every diplomatic imbroglio and military confrontation in the Middle East had occurred under the shadow of the global rivalry between the United States and the Soviet Union; in 1990, the two powers acted as friends rather than as adversaries, reviving hopes for the United Nations that had been all but abandoned during the years of the cold war, and in circumstances that were far more auspicious than those existing when the United Nations was founded.

This was a very strong position for the allied forces. It did not guarantee Iraq's immediate withdrawal from Kuwait; it did, however, protect each of the values and interests—world order, regional security, and the global economy—that the administration insistently, but implausibly, said could be protected only if Iraq immediately evacuated Kuwait.

Could such a posture have been maintained indefinitely? Many observers held that it could not have been, that a strategy of punitive containment would have broken down over time. On this view, the difficulty with sanctions was not that they were ineffective but that over time they could not be maintained; the difficulty with military containment was not that it was powerless but that at some point the protective force would have to be removed; and the difficulty with the diplomatic coalition was not that it was unimpressive or failed to confer real benefits but that it would fall apart over time and allow Saddam Hussein to proclaim a victory.

★ ★ ★

In considering the danger that American military forces could not stay in Saudi Arabia indefinitely, there were two main possibilities. One was that the Saudi government would change its mind, the other that this government would be overthrown. While one could not say that either prospect was a mathematical impossibility, nevertheless, certain features of the situation made either prospect highly unlikely.

When the Saudi government invited American forces onto its territory, it knew that it was breaching a highly significant barrier. For a decade it had been besieged by voices across the Persian Gulf denouncing America as the living incarnation of Satan, and claiming that the Saudi government was complicit in spreading his devilish deeds on earth. For much more than a decade, it had watched with alarm as the United States adopted a closer relationship with Israel. Verbal remonstrances of the Israelis by the United States were accompanied by ever greater levels of financial aid; the American-Israeli relationship, though always under some strain, always endured. Arabs who looked upon Israel's very existence as an alien intrusion on the Arab nation, or who saw a profound religious insult in Israel's continued possession of some of Islam's holiest shrines, knew that the United States was an earnest and powerful supporter of the Jewish state. Certainly the Saudis knew this. They could have had no expectation that

122   America's decision to protect Saudi Arabia entailed a decision to abandon Israel.

Despite the disadvantages of identifying itself so completely with the United States, Saudi Arabia had little alternative to doing so. By itself, Saudi Arabia was no match for the military power that Iraq disposed. Its 65,000-man army was little better than a police force; its air force, though well equipped, was too small to contend with Iraq alone. By his invasion of Kuwait, Saddam Hussein had shown himself to be an implacable foe of his former benefactors. Under these circumstances, the Saudis had no alternative but to accept an offer of American protection. Their survival was at stake in a direct and immediate sense. This was a powerful motive; there is no reason for thinking that it would have been felt with less force by the Saudis so long as Iraq posed a threat to its survival.

The possibility remained that the Saudi government might be overthrown. The issue, Henry Kissinger said in November, was not American staying power but the host country's domestic stability. It was not only Saudi Arabia that would be threatened with internal upheaval in the event of a failure by the United States to secure an immediate Iraqi withdrawal from Kuwait. All American-aligned governments in the region—Kissinger specifically mentioned Egypt, Morocco, and Turkey—would also be gravely threatened and probably swept away by waves of Islamic fundamentalism and anti-Western fervor.

The image of the Arab world Kissinger evoked was a popular one in the United States. Indeed, it was an image that the opponents of the war also in large measure shared. On this view, the regimes that ruled in the Middle East had no more staying power than the barren earth on top of a rumbling volcano. If we used force, said the doves, the regimes would be blown away. If we failed to use force, said the hawks, the regimes would topple.

The presumption of profound instability evoked by both the supporters and opponents of war was curious for a simple reason: contrary to the common presumption of a profoundly unstable political culture, the Arab political world had in fact enjoyed extraordinary stability over the previous two decades. The proverbial observer who had gone into hibernation at the end of 1970 **123** would have awakened to find, in 1990, the same ruling groups in power among all the major Arab states. The Baath still ruled in Syria and Iraq, the Hashemites in Jordan. No gulf monarchy had been seriously threatened by internal upheaval, much less overthrown by it. Sadat was dead, but the men he had brought into the ruling circle remained in charge.

This stability could hardly be considered as accidental, the product of a bizarre and misleading coincidence. It stemmed, on the contrary, from the adoption of highly effective methods of political rule. The 1960s had shown that it was dangerous to allow potential challengers to acquire an independent base of power; this could be prevented. It was dangerous to allow men to speak freely; they must be watched. Every state acquired an extensive internal security apparatus; most employed torture. The methods by which Saddam Hussein maintained his power were only an extreme manifestation of a common tendency. The Westerner might avert his eyes from these rough methods, or lament the relative absence of civilized standards of governance. It could not be said that such methods were just; it could be said, for it was obvious, that they were highly effective.

The Saudis employed the same methods of stifling dissent as were common elsewhere in the Arab world. Their position was secured even more by the fact that to the threat of death and persecution they were able to add the inducements of material welfare—inducements that, by virtue of the riches at their disposal, they employed on a large scale. Unlike the poorer Arab states, they faced no *lumpenproletariat*; indeed, they hardly needed to worry about the formation of a proletariat, since the hard work in their societies was done by imported laborers that were easily dispensable and might be deported without a second thought.

None of this means that the presence over a protracted period of Western forces of the size that were committed would not have been disruptive to Saudi society. If the visions of Islamic fundamentalists sweeping away the House of Saud were highly implausible, it was nevertheless the case that such a large scale presence of American forces, even if largely isolated from contact with the

124   local population, made the Saudis nervous. Indeed, it made Americans nervous as well. The prospect of large American ground forces, including many reservists, encamped forever in a bleak and inhospitable environment appeared distinctively unattractive. But these objections apply only to the force that was initially sent (and even more so, of course, to the force that was doubled). They are hardly applicable to the reduced force, centered on airpower, that might have been sent to sustain a policy of punitive containment. Such a force, while perfectly adequate for defensive purposes, would have posed no more of a danger to Saudi rule than the large colonies of Americans who have long played a central role in the running of the Saudi oil industry.

The war showed that the critics of the administration's policy had greatly exaggerated the danger of convulsive upheavals in the Middle East as a result of the decision to use force against Iraq. It did not demonstrate, however, the converse position held by the proponents of the war—that the failure to use force would have led to such upheavals. Both sides in this debate, it may reasonably be concluded, were guilty of gross exaggerations. But if the exigencies of political debate led in this instance, as they normally do, to marked exaggeration and even caricature, the question still remained significant. The proponents of the war could argue, not without plausibility, that our coalition partners would have concluded that forbearance and restraint on the part of the United States stemmed from fear and cowardice. They could also argue that the Arab masses hated us anyway; the use of force would make them fear us. Neither of these contentions could be dismissed out of hand, for both contained a measure of truth. The case for the opposition, on the other hand, rested on the assumption that Arab elites, disgruntled over the putative lack of manliness in American policy, would not have broken with us over the issue, for they had nowhere else to go. This case rested also on the assumptions that hatred and resentment in the Arab and Moslem world toward the West are matters of degree, that the massive use of force against an Arab country entailing widespread devastation and loss of life would induce not only fear but also greatly heightened levels of resentment, and that the latter would remain to plague American policy in the region even as the former dissipated. The issue was as

old as politics itself; it could scarcely be resolved on the basis of a   **125**
year's experience. If the immediate consequences of the war,
which fostered a kind of stunned immobility in the Arab world,
appeared to bear out the case of the hawks, the long-term consequences may yet strengthen the case of the doves.

★ ★ ★

The most insistent fears raised by the advocates of an early resolution of the crisis were that the international coalition the Bush
administration had assembled at the United Nations and in the
Middle East would fall apart. These fears tended to be general and
abstract, not specific and concrete. They came in two main
varieties. One fear was that the United States would not be able to
sustain over time a coalition that could keep the sanctions in
place; the other fear was that it would be impossible to sustain any
consensus in international society for the use of force against Iraq.

The danger that the diplomatic coalition on behalf of economic sanctions would fall apart was always grossly exaggerated by
the advocates of war. The dangers to this coalition were minimal.
The authority to make the embargo on Iraqi exports and imports
militarily effective was granted by the Security Council at an early
stage of the crisis; to reverse these UN authorizing resolutions
required the vote of the United States. From a strictly legal point
of view, the United States enjoyed the authority to maintain the
sanctions indefinitely so long as Iraq refused compliance with the
UN resolutions; from a military point of view, it also enjoyed the
power to do so.

The effectiveness of the sanctions rested preeminently on the
ability to deny Iraq the revenue it had traditionally received from
oil exports. So long as the export embargo held, the import
embargo would be largely self-enforcing. This, at least, would have
been the case after Iraq exhausted the cash reserves it had on hand
and the gold it seized in Kuwait. The legions of smugglers who
might step into the breach and defeat the aims of the embargo
required an incentive to do so; without revenue, Iraq could provide no such incentive. The fact that Turkey and Iran had long
borders with Iraq that made it difficult to close off entirely well-

126   established trade routes was true, but irrelevant. The fact that international arms merchants existed who would trade with anyone, and who might be capable of escaping detection from the embargo's enforcers, was also true, and equally irrelevant. Trade requires reciprocity; without revenue, Iraq would have little to give.

Nor was it the case that the burdens the embargo inflicted on consumer countries were insupportable. These burdens, as it happened, were greater than they need have been: a determined use of strategic petroleum reserves at the outset of the crisis would have set sharp bounds to the price increases that occurred.* More generally, the burdens that ensued from the embargo fell precisely where they should have fallen: on consumers of oil. The embargo enforced a kind of burden sharing in the crisis that was closely related to the measures states had taken before the crisis to curb the consumption or increase the domestic production of energy. Some states—in Eastern Europe, for example—were hit especially hard by the price increases; the Turks lost revenue from the closure of the Iraqi pipeline through their country. At the same time, enough money was raised during the crisis, both from the threatened oil producers in the gulf as well as from the advanced industrialized democracies, to mitigate much of the pain these states suffered. (A smaller American deployment to the gulf, in fact, would have freed up revenues for precisely these purposes.)

Nor was it the case that the embargo was unsustainable because it would have produced such widespread suffering in Iraq that there would be irresistible pressures to lift it. For the embargo to achieve its purposes, it was not necessary to induce famine or to cause a widespread health crisis in Iraq. The UN resolution au-

---

* "Price explosions," as M.A. Adelman notes, "are rooted in individuals' fears of shortage. Their fright is rational, but can be prevented. The SPR needs to be a seller of last resort, to assure buyers a constant ready supply. Prevention of precautionary and speculative overbuying will prevent panic and prevent or moderate price increases in oil markets, just as the Federal Reserve System prevents panic in money markets. Had the SPR been used early on in the Gulf crisis, there would have been little panic demand. There might have been a mild and reversible price rise, but no explosion." "Oil Fallacies," *Foreign Policy*, Spring 1991, p. 13.

thorizing sanctions had, in fact, specifically excluded these objectives. Though there was clearly a tension between the desire to deprive Saddam of his financial base and the desirability of limiting the suffering of Iraq's civilian population, it does not thereby follow that a sanctions policy that sought to avoid famine or health epidemics would have failed. Nor do these considerations justify the conclusion that, given the humanitarian issues the embargo undoubtedly raised, military action was more humane than a policy of sanctions. The cumulative effects of the destruction of Iraq's infrastructure during the war appear to be substantially in excess, from a humanitarian point of view, of the pain likely to have been inflicted by sanctions.

Even with the legal authority and military power to maintain sanctions indefinitely, it might still be argued that the United States would have at some point faced powerful political pressures to lift the embargo short of a satisfactory settlement. To show the seriousness of this danger, however, it is not enough to say that the Soviet Union or France would have been satisfied with a resolution of the crisis that fell somewhat short of U.S. demands. This was undoubtedly the case. It hardly means, however, that either the Soviet Union or France would have been able to raise a diplomatic coalition in support of Iraq in opposition to the United States, thus creating overwhelming diplomatic pressures on the American government to accept a settlement that it considered dangerous or unacceptable. Such a prospect was wholly unlikely. Even if many governments agreed with the Soviet or French position, they would have supported the United States anyway. The coalition had been brought into being in the first place not primarily because of the duty that all states felt toward the great principles of international society but because of the deference that most states felt it prudent to give to American power. In theory, the existence of the coalition was a dramatic fulfillment of the aspirations of the advocates of collective security; in fact, it was a testament to America's hegemonial position.

The principal danger that the coalition would fall apart was posed by the administration's determination to threaten war. This did indeed make many states nervous. Outside the Middle East,

128 few states wanted a war. In the Soviet Union, the prospect of a massive use of American force near the southern border of the Soviet Union, and against a state with which the Soviet Union had previously enjoyed close relations, made the remnants of the old guard deeply resentful at their new-found status as an American supplicant. Shevardnadze's willingness to support this course of action, and the internal opposition it aroused, was one of the principal factors in his resignation in late December. In all likelihood, Gorbachev himself agreed to the November 29 UN resolution authorizing the use of force only because he considered it vital to maintain good relations with the United States, and not out of any belief that it was the wisest course of action under the circumstances. A similar calculation was evident among the Germans and the Japanese.

In the event, the reservations that many states felt over American actions in the crisis proved virtually irrelevant. For some, such as Germany and France, the reservations themselves vanished with the outbreak of the war, which proved to be popular with most Europeans. For others, such as the Soviet Union, the reservations intensified with the outbreak of hostilities, but such reservations were incapable of deflecting the Bush administration from its course of action. In the days before the ground offensive began, the Soviet Union reached agreement with Iraq on a plan for settling the crisis. This was ignored. The plain meaning of the Soviet-Iraqi agreement was that the coalition had fallen apart; even so, it did not affect the ability of the United States to pursue the course it deemed appropriate.

A separate set of anxieties for the fate of the coalition centered on the unpredictable character of Middle Eastern politics. The coalition was unnatural in that it joined states that had previously been mortal enemies and might become so again. For the chief supporter and benefactor of Israel to stand at the head of the same coalition of Arab states that had fought Israel in 1973 was unusual. The incident at Temple Mount, during which Israeli policemen had fired on stone-throwing Palestinian demonstrators, killing nineteen, was a painful reminder of this fact, and caused a few embarrassing moments at the UN for the United States. But it scarcely caused a fracturing of the coalition against Iraq, and there were strong reasons for believing similar incidents would not do so **129** in the future. However much our Arab coalition partners may have regretted the intimacy of relations between the United States and Israel, they went into the coalition against Iraq for reasons of their own, and with the knowledge that American-Israeli ties were not likely to be broken. The Saudis needed American protection; the Egyptians required American (and Saudi) money; the Syrians, having been abandoned by their previous benefactor (the Soviet Union), were looking to make themselves useful to the gulf states. They all hated Saddam Hussein. Each had good and substantial reasons for remaining in the coalition whatever the future brought in the way of heightened tensions between Israel and the Palestinians.

★　★　★

The pressures faced by the Bush administration for a rapid resolution to the crisis did not stem from the danger that the coalition would fall apart; they stemmed instead from American domestic politics. The great danger was not that a policy of punitive containment would fail to protect American vital interests; it was that it threatened to complicate greatly the president's political position at home. A protracted stand-off of a year or more, which it seemed well within Saddam Hussein's power to produce, would be debilitating. It would push the crisis into the 1992 presidential election year and might even revive the charges, which the president greatly resented, that he was a wimp.

The 1990 midterm elections provided a foretaste of this danger. In the run-up to the elections, the president suffered a precipitous drop in popularity in the opinion polls, the proximate cause of which was his endorsement of a budget agreement with a bipartisan coalition of Republican and Democratic congressional leaders. The agreement provoked a rebellion in the rank and file of both parties. Liberal Democrats, who supported sharper reductions in military spending than the agreement called for, were unwilling to support the agreement's near total endorsement of the president's military program; far more serious from the president's vantage point, congressional Republicans were aghast at the abandonment of the pledge—"no new taxes"—that had carried Bush to victory in 1988. As the government teetered on the edge

130   of a shutdown in operations, the public recoiled from the impression of ungovernability produced by the political disarray. The Republican victory in the elections, which had been confidently expected only a few months before, vanished amid a sudden surge of public disillusionment and anger.

The comparison between Bush's conduct in the budget imbroglio and his handling of the Iraqi crisis was not lost on many observers. In the immediate aftermath of Saddam Hussein's invasion of Kuwait on August 2, 1990, President Bush pledged that the conquest would not stand, but he had apparently embraced a strategy for contending with the crisis—military containment and economic sanctions—that held out little promise of an imminent Iraqi withdrawal from Kuwait. Neoconservative columnists asked whether the president's abandonment of his pledge on taxes was a foretaste of his readiness to abandon his pledge on Kuwait. The same disposition that had led the president to reach out to his domestic opponents on the budget might make him equally willing to reach out and compromise with the opponents of war, whether at home or abroad. Critics from the right painted the picture of a president immobilized by his search for consensus, and the very qualities that earned the president praise from liberals— preeminently his stress on UN approval for his effort to isolate and contain Iraq—were seen by neoconservatives as the harbinger of a strategy that would fail to secure Iraq's withdrawal from Kuwait and leave it in a position to secure hegemony over the Persian Gulf. The very factors that had led to Jimmy Carter's crushing defeat in 1980—a reputation for inconsistency and appeasement, a foreign crisis that left the initiative to the adversary and was a daily reminder of the limits of American power, and incessant and enfeebling attacks from the right—seemed in prospect for George Bush.

It was against this background, in late October, that the president decided to double the size of American forces and to move toward a showdown with Iraq. In doing so, he sensed, with some justification, that a protracted crisis would inevitably redound to the benefit of the Democrats, even if the party's leadership made no direct attacks on him. He saw about him alarming signs of economic deterioration, including a sharp collapse in **131** consumer confidence, for which he would inevitably be blamed. Above all, he feared that a protracted stalemate would fatally undermine a reputation for decisive leadership that he wished dearly to solidify. Though punitive containment would leave Saddam Hussein with an offer that he could not refuse in the long run, he showed every indication that he would refuse it in the short run, and this was enough to doom it in the president's eyes. The balance achieved in the gulf would not balance at home. There wasn't time for it politically.

CHAPTER 11

Justice and the War

The conclusion that the war was unnecessary to protect American interests in world order, regional security, or the global economy, that a policy of punitive containment offered to vindicate all American interests of material and permanent importance, and that such a policy might have been pursued indefinitely with little risk, does not lead inexorably to the conclusion that the war was unjust. Even if the gulf war is judged to have been unnecessary to secure American vital interests, it nevertheless met some of the requirements of a just war. Whether it met all of these requirements, as the administration (and many moralists) argued at the time, is, however, another question.

The eternal need to justify action is perhaps never more apparent than when nations resort to force. The interests that prompt states to go to war are seldom, if ever, considered sufficient as a justification of a course that entails the taking of lives and the destruction of property. Beyond the appeal to interest and necessity, there is also the appeal to justice. In the tradition of the West, this appeal has invoked standards set long ago by the great theologians of the Church, standards that in turn were followed by writers on the law of nations. Characterized as "just war" doctrine, these standards have embodied the essential convictions of a civilization on the relationship between war and justice. That they were invoked by President Bush in the course of the gulf war cannot occasion surprise. In one form or another, they have been regularly appealed to by the nation's statesmen in resorting to **133** force. *

In justifying the use of force in the gulf, President Bush placed the greatest weight on the indisputable fact that America was responding to a clear-cut case of aggression across borders. In focusing on Iraq's aggression, the president was following a well-marked path. In the American tradition, the justice or injustice of war has turned primarily upon the circumstances immediately attending the initiation of force. The just war is the war waged in self-defense or in collective defense against an armed attack. Conversely, the unjust war is the war initiated in circumstances other than those of self- or collective defense against armed aggression. The American view of the just war has thus been characterized by a singular preoccupation with the overt act of resorting to force. It has proceeded from the conviction that whatever a state's grievances, aggressive war is an unjust—and illegal—means for settling those grievances. This conviction was given full expression in the gulf war.

The restriction of the just war to the war of self- or collective defense against armed aggression corresponds to the twentieth century reconstruction of the Christian doctrine of *bellum justum.* In the classic version of the doctrine, the just war was a war of execution, an act of vindictive justice, taken to punish a state for a wrong done and unamended. But the rights in defense of which states might resort to war, in the absence of satisfactory alternative means of redress, were not restricted to that of self-defense.

In the twentieth century reconstruction, however, war is no longer a means generally permitted to states for the redress of rights that have been violated. Still less is war considered a legitimate means for changing the status quo. Armed force remains a means permitted to states only as a measure of defense against unjust attack. This restriction of the just war rests in the main on the presumption—indeed, conviction—that war no longer

---

* "Justice," as Burke held, "is the great standing policy of civil society; and any eminent departure from it, under any circumstances, lies under the suspicion of being no policy at all." (Edmund Burke, *Reflections on the Revolution in France* [Indianapolis: Bobbs-Merrill, 1959], p. 180.)

134   serves as an apt and proportionate means for resolving international conflicts. International law has followed a similar course. The *bellum legale*, as the *bellum justum*, is now substantially limited to one of defense, individual or collective, against armed attack.

This far-reaching change in the right of recourse to war has not gone without dissent. Even so, the international consensus on limiting the just cause of war to that of self- or collective defense against aggression is clear. That consensus was reaffirmed in the course of the crisis that led to war in the Persian Gulf. A war of collective defense undertaken in response to a textbook act of aggression, the justice of its cause was apparent.

That a war is undertaken in a just cause does not ensure that it is a just war. In the American view, there is a strong disposition to assume a necessary relationship not only between the justice of resorting to war and the purposes sought in war but also between the causes and purposes of war and the manner of waging war. Moral indifference to the manner of employing force is the result of moral certainty respecting the causes of, and purposes sought in, war. Just war doctrine teaches otherwise. It emphasizes that even a defensive war is not of necessity a just war. The requirements laid down by just war doctrine that the conduct of war must conform to the principles of discrimination and of proportionality apply to those waging a defensive war. The justice of war's cause does not excuse the injustice of war's conduct. If the latter is sufficiently grave, it may morally taint a war undertaken with just cause. Even a defensive war, then, may become an unjust war if it is marked by the deliberate attack upon noncombatants or if the good secured by such war is clearly outweighed by the evil attendant upon its conduct.

If these considerations hold for a war that is clearly defensive in both cause and purpose, they are all the more relevant for a war the purposes of which go well beyond those of defense, conventionally defined. A war that is clearly defensive in cause may be much less so in purpose. Indeed, the same purposes and anticipations that inform a preventive war may also inform a war presumably fought in self-defense. An essentially defensive war leaves the power and position of the enemy substantially unchanged. Purpose

is limited to repelling the aggressor, not to destroying him. But it
may be argued that merely to repel the aggression that gave rise to
self-defense, rather than to removing the source of aggression, is
insufficient for even strictly defensive purposes given the circumstances that continue to characterize international society.
Within civil society the state presumably assures that an aggressor
once repelled will be removed. In international society, the same
assurance cannot be given to states. An equally severe restriction
of measures taken in self-defense may well prove unreasonable in
that it may defeat the essential purpose for which such measures
are considered justified in the first place. This familiar argument
has evident merit. Yet its acceptance carries an equally evident
risk, for it is in effect a license to expand the purposes of a war
begun in defense to a point where it may become very difficult to
set meaningful limits to the exercise of self- or collective defense.
As these purposes expand, so will the interpretation belligerents
give the criterion of proportionality that serves to justify the acts
taken in their name.

It is with these general admonitions in mind that we may ask:
Was the gulf war a just war in the manner in which it was waged?
Were the means chosen apt and proportionate? Did the good
secured by the war clearly outweigh the evil attendant upon its
conduct?

The manner in which the war was waged reflected, in the first
instance, the vast disparity in the means available to the two sides.
This disparity meant that the element of reciprocity was largely
absent from the conflict. The expectation that like will be returned for like has always been the most important constraint on
the conduct of war. In the gulf war, the side possessed of enormous
technological advantage could act almost without fear of enemy
reprisal.

The conduct of the war also reflected the conditions placed
on the use of force by a public that would not tolerate another
Vietnam. A war in the gulf, the president accordingly promised
the nation, would not be "protracted"; the American government
would not permit "our troops to have their hands tied behind their
backs"; there would not be "any murky ending." Nor would Amer-

136   ican forces remain "a single day" longer than was necessary to achieve the objective the administration sought.[1] These commitments could be honored only by a war marked by the application of force on a massive scale, with the objective of utterly overwhelming the adversary and destroying his capabilities to commit further aggression. Merely to drive Saddam from Kuwait, though leaving his military power intact, would not remove the danger of future aggression. Finally, these objectives had to be achieved at a modest price in American lives; if the price of victory was substantial casualties it was likely to prove too high for a nation that until the very eve of armed conflict remained deeply divided over the wisdom of going to war.

The war that resulted from these conditioning circumstances was waged with extraordinary ferocity. The costs of the war in human lives remain obscure, in part because neither the Iraqi nor the American government has an interest in determining and publicizing these costs and in part because civilian casualties will continue to mount for some time to come, if only because the human effects of the physical destruction visited on Iraq have yet to run their course. When the full costs in lives are finally calculated, combatant and noncombatant deaths may well number several hundred thousand. To this grim statistic must of course be added the vast destruction of the industrial plant in Iraq, a destruction undertaken in part in the name of immediate military necessity and in part in pursuit of the larger objective of eliminating Iraq as a regional power.

These and still other costs of the war may not be lightly passed over in considering its justice. Political and military leaders habitually employ a peculiar moral arithmetic in calculating the costs of war, in which the moral total of such costs largely depends upon the identity of those whose lives are being counted, but moralists are expected to assess war's costs with a measure of impartiality. From Washington's perspective, the moral costs of the war against Iraq appear quite modest. Viewed from a more impartial perspective, a very different judgment may be reached. Indeed, had the total casualties in the war been roughly the same but more equally shared, it is altogether likely that this nation's judgment—political and moral—would be very different from the **137** prevailing judgment today.

These considerations notwithstanding, did the manner in which the gulf war was waged satisfy the requirements of discrimination and of proportionality? Of the two requirements, the principle forbidding the direct and intentional attack on the civilian population has generally been considered the more significant. The distinction between those who may and may not be made the object of attack is held in *bellum justum* to define the essential difference between war and murder—between the permitted and the forbidden taking of human life. The deliberate killing of the innocent is always to be avoided, even as a measure of reprisal in response to similar measures of an adversary. Indiscriminate warfare, moreover, is almost by definition total war, and total war is very difficult to reconcile with the other general principle regulating war's conduct, that of proportionality.

In the gulf war, a considerable effort was made to avoid direct attacks on Iraq's civilian population. That effort appears to have been quite successful, a success made possible in part by the precision of the weapons employed to destroy targets proximate to the civilian population. At the same time, there has been a substantial, and still growing, number of civilian deaths that are the indirect result of allied air strikes. In bombing what were designated as military objectives, facilities that sustained civilian life were also destroyed. The severe disabling of Iraq's electrical power grid, to cite perhaps the most prominent example, was undertaken to impede the enemy's communications. It has also, however, contributed to undermining the public health system, the electric grid forming a key part of that system, which has led in turn to inadequate sanitation and, ultimately, to epidemics.

It has been contended that these, and similar, effects of the bombing were beside the intention of the actors, even if they were in some measure foreseen, and that the death and injury of noncombatants did not constitute a means for achieving an otherwise legitimate military end. Provided these requirements of *bellum justum* are satisfied, there remains only the requirement of proportionality—that the evil effects not outweigh the good effects—in order to give

138   moral sanction to the air attacks on Iraq. But the difficulties that have
so often been raised in the past by bombing are in large measure also
raised in the present case. What are termed collateral effects may
reach a point at which it becomes very difficult to consider these
effects as being beside the intention of the actors. Inevitably, there is
a point where one must deduce intent from effects or consequences,
the determination of that point being, in turn, dependent largely on
quantitative considerations. In practice, then, whether the death
and injury done to the innocent is intended or not is determined by
the scope of this death and injury. Even though there are no
objective criteria for determining how much death and injury may be
done to the innocent while still preserving the right intention, this
cannot affect the judgment that such criteria exists. Whether these
criteria were breached in the recent war is an issue that is yet to be
persuasively addressed.

The view has nevertheless arisen that the advent of precision-guided weapons has alleviated the hitherto almost intractable
issues attending efforts to reconcile the principle of discrimination
with the conduct of modern warfare. On this view, the war against
Iraq foreshadows a time when the use of such weapons may no
longer result in collateral damage as understood in the past. The
destruction of military objectives may then be undertaken without
any concurrent death or injury to the civilian population. Even so,
this would not of necessity mean that the requirement of discrimination had been satisfied; it might only mean that the time and
manner in which noncombatants were put at mortal risk had
changed. As the gulf war has demonstrated, provided only that
military objectives are given a sufficiently broad definition, the
immunity belligerents are obliged to afford noncombatants may be
threatened quite as gravely as it was in earlier wars of this century.
The conclusion seems unavoidable that discrimination in war will
continue to depend less on the precision of weapons, or, for that
matter, on the care with which they are employed against military
objectives, than on the scope and meaning that is given to military necessity (and hence to the determination of what constitutes
a legitimate military objective). If this conclusion has merit, it
suggests that rather than enabling belligerents to wage clearly

discriminate warfare, the principal significance of precision- **139**
guided weapons might instead be to permit belligerents to wage
indiscriminate warfare while persuading themselves that they are
acting in a highly discriminate manner. The gulf war indicated
that this delusion may already have taken a firm hold.

In the end, the justice of the gulf war must turn on the test of
proportionality. Proportionality provides the critical test for judging
virtually every major aspect of the war, including whether the requirement of discrimination was met. If the conduct of the war is
considered to have satisfied the requirement of discrimination, it did
so largely because it presumably met the requirement of proportionality as well. The criterion of discrimination is satisfied when the
evil represented by the death and injury of noncombatants is not
deemed disproportionate to the good otherwise served by the war.

The principle requiring that the values preserved through
force must be proportionate to the values sacrificed through force
is admittedly little more than a counsel of prudence. It expresses
the common sense of the matter. When war becomes dispropor-
tionately destructive to the good it serves, it must be condemned.
Judgments of proportionality, and its converse, are necessarily
very rough and subject to considerable uncertainty. Still, they are
indispensable if war is to be regarded as a rational and moral
activity. These judgments express what may be termed the "logic
of justification" and it is quite difficult to imagine how meaningful
moral discourse about war could be undertaken without them.

In the conduct of the gulf war the issue of proportionality also
arose as a result of the huge disparity in combatant casualties
suffered by the respective sides. Is proportionality violated when a
belligerent takes a multitude of the enemy's lives in order to save,
or simply not to put at risk, a few of his own? That this was done in
the recent war is clear. In doing so, military commanders invoked
the plea of military necessity as justification for their actions.
Given the indeterminate character of military necessity, the appeal to it often appeared plausible. Even so, there are surely
limits—ill-defined though they may be—to the number of enemy
lives that may justifiably be taken to avoid risking however small a
number of one's own. At some point, the imperious claims of

140   military necessity must yield to the claims of humanity, even if it is conceded—a concession the moralist may make only at his peril—that although human lives are human lives some lives are still more important than others. That point, it would seem, is above all dependent on quantitative considerations.

Was that point exceeded in the gulf war? The question has only seldom been raised. When it has, more often than not the response has been to shift the meaning of military necessity from its narrower operational sense to its broader political-strategic sense. In the latter sense, military necessity is above all a function of the objectives sought in war, of the purposes or ends for which a war is fought, rather than simply the immediate requirements of military operations (as well as the means available to belligerents for effectively carrying out these operations). Partiality in the conduct of war is accordingly transformed into impartiality when judged by the purposes or ends of war. Once these purposes are endowed with enough significance, military necessity may serve to justify behavior that is very one-sided in its human consequences.

In the gulf war, what moral embarrassment was felt at the disproportion in casualties suffered by the respective sides was partially relieved by invoking the larger ends of the war. Yet it was not so much the ends of the war that strained the principle of proportionality to a breaking point as it was the manner in which the nation and its government were determined from the outset to wage war. That manner would likely have found the expression it did whatever the purposes given for the war, for it reflected the conditions upon which public support rested.

These considerations do not establish that the manner in which the war was waged made it an unjust war. No such demonstration can be made, for there is, in the end, no clear basis on which to weigh the good preserved or restored by the war, beginning with Kuwait's independence as a sovereign state, against the evil effects it undoubtedly brought. It may be said with greater confidence, however, that its conduct resulted in deplorable consequences which cannot simply be shrugged off as the unfortunate though inevitable by-product of war. These consequences seriously tainted the conduct of the war. Nor can it be said, in mitigation, that they were unforeseen and unintended. Quite the **141** contrary, to an extent greater than most wars, the consequences of this war were foreseen and intended. Determined not to have more than the most modest casualties, intent on not getting into a quagmire, enjoying great technological advantages, and persuaded that the adversary was essentially unredeemable, the only reasonable expectation was that the kind of war would be waged that in fact was waged. Those who led the nation into war left little doubt on this score by the statements they made prior to the war's outbreak. The generals presiding over the strategy and conduct of the war warned Baghdad that a war, once begun, would be waged with "unprecedented ferocity" and would result in the "killing" of the Iraqi army. The president broadened the warning to the people of Iraq for whom war, he declared, would be a "calamity." [2] And so it proved to be.

That the war which followed these warnings raises grave questions about its conduct is perhaps less sobering than the realization that it was virtually the only kind of war we could have waged given the outlook of the American military establishment and the nation at large. The disproportionality that marked the conduct of the war has deep roots, which gave to its conduct an almost inexorable character. The consequences of the gulf war have given new support to the view that the circumstances in which war remains an "apt and proportionate" and, accordingly, a just means have further narrowed. In doing so, the gulf conflict has given a new dimension to the just war requirement that war is a "last resort," to be undertaken only after all alternative means of redress have been tried in vain. Urged during the crisis by those favoring the continuation of sanctions as a means of dislodging Iraq from Kuwait, that requirement appeared irrelevant to many in view of Iraq's aggression. Yet even the right of collective defense against aggression is not unconditioned, particularly in circumstances where an alternative means of redress holds out a reasonable prospect of ultimate success. In these circumstances, the obligation of last resort must be measured against the expectation of war's destructiveness. In the gulf crisis, that obligation was not given the weight it deserved.

CHAPTER 12

The Responsibilities
of Victory

The decision to go to war has long been recognized as among the most serious and portentous that a nation can make. Though it may, in crucial respects, represent merely the continuation of politics by other means, it may also lead to a set of circumstances so radically different from those existing before the onset of hostilities as to require sharp adaptations in policy and objectives. Even if the view is taken, therefore, that the gulf war was unnecessary to vindicate American vital interests, the question of whether American war aims were wisely chosen would still remain. Though American objectives while at peace might have been sensibly limited to what was necessary to secure our vital interests, it does not follow that, once at war, the attempt to limit American objectives was equally wise. In peace, the obligation of the statesman is to preserve the advantages of that state as far as possible without sacrificing vital interests; in war, his obligation is to act to ensure that the use of force creates the conditions under which a durable peace can be constructed.

This obligation is particularly evident in circumstances of a lopsided victory or total defeat. Under such conditions, the victor normally enjoys a freedom of action to shape the conditions of the peace that is utterly out of the reach of the defeated power. It is a freedom of action, moreover, that is not available to any of the belligerents if conflict ends in a wary standoff. Overwhelming victory or superiority, then, is a special condition. In the Western political tradition, at least, this condition has normally been thought, by philosophers and statesmen alike, to confer not only

rights but also duties. The morality peculiar to this kind of rela-   **143**
tionship was once a topic of absorbing interest in the Western
tradition, since it rested upon an assumption of fundamental
inequality among human beings. The relations of master and
slave, of parent and child, of civilized to uncivilized nation, of
superior to inferior, were reinforcing aspects of an inquiry that
reached into every area of human life from antiquity to modern
times. Only in the twentieth century, whose ethos found the
assumption of inequality offensive and which considered specula-
tions proceeding from this premise the means by which the powerful mystified and oppressed the weak, has the topic lost the interest
that it once excited. But the question, once so absorbing in ages of
vast empires and vast inequalities, is not less relevant today.

Indeed, the inquiry is especially pertinent in the present
instance, since it was partially owing to an avowed adherence to
the fundamental assumption of the equality of states that the
United States refused to do what those who achieve total victory
normally do—occupy the defeated country and impose a pacification upon it. The desire of the Bush administration to avoid a
protracted commitment in the gulf was an important factor in the
shaping of American war aims, for it made it imperative to smash
Iraqi power as completely as possible. It made it equally imperative
to stand aside while Saddam crushed the risings of the Shi'a and
the Kurds. The desire to avoid an occupation, in other words, was
responsible in great part for those aspects of the war that call most
into question America's observance of the principles of proportionality and discrimination, and thereby lend credence to the
charge that the war launched by the administration, considered in
its full aspect, was unjust. The desire to avoid an occupation was
equally responsible for the charges of bad faith and inhumanity
that arose when, after having called for the people of Iraq to
depose Saddam Hussein, the administration watched passively as
Saddam Hussein crushed the Kurdish and Shi'a rebellions.

These considerations support the conclusion that it was morally incumbent on the United States to attempt to ensure the
pacification and rehabilitation of Iraq in the aftermath of the war.
This obligation followed not only from the fact of overwhelming

144 victory as such but also from the severe damage inflicted on Iraq's infrastructure during the war and because of President Bush's call for the people of Iraq to rise up and depose Saddam. The discharge of this obligation, in turn, would have meant military operations that sought the forcible removal of Saddam Hussein from power, entailing the temporary occupation of Baghdad by U.S. and allied forces, and the installation of a moderately democratic regime that would have allowed for the reconstruction of Iraq's economy and the rehabilitation of the Iraqi state.

This conclusion does not rest on a presumed duty to bring, even through force if necessary, the blessings of democratic government to peoples suffering under despotic governments. Considered as a general matter, the United States has neither the duty nor the right to undertake such interventions. It rests instead on the consideration that the war itself constituted a massive intervention in Iraqi affairs. Once this intervention was effected, the great question then became not whether but how to pursue a policy of intervention. The course chosen by the Bush administration inflicted a great deal of hardship on the Iraqi civilian population; it also left the Kurdish and Shi'a rebels to an exceedingly grim fate. Whether considered from the standpoint of justice, or of good faith, or of humanity, the course pursued by the administration was one that entailed serious moral liabilities.

It may be acknowledged that a different military strategy would have considerably lessened these obligations; that had the United States refrained from destroying Iraq's infrastructure and had it not called for the overthrow of Saddam by the people of Iraq, the weight of the obligation to reconstruct and rehabilitate would have been considerably lessened. At the same time, however, such an alternative strategy was neither followed nor even seriously considered. Indeed, American policy was marked throughout by the conviction that the victor owed nothing to the defeated state, and that whatever we did or did not do it was Saddam Hussein who deserved the blame.

The occupation and pacification of Iraq would have carried with it several ancillary advantages: it would have allowed American forces to root out and destroy Iraq's infrastructure and stockpiles of ABC weapons and components, and it would have brought **145** the swift demise of Saddam Hussein. The administration sought to achieve both of these objectives at the end of the war through a continuation of economic sanctions, but in circumstances of disease and famine that made the policy a cruel and unusual punishment. Iraq's refusal to acquiesce in the terms providing for limited oil sales led to an impasse that severely exacerbated the health and food crisis in the country. A policy intent on occupation and pacification would have avoided these conundrums.

Finally, and perhaps most importantly, a policy of occupation and pacification would have given the use of American force a positive purpose. In contrast to the Bush administration's policy, which invoked both order and liberty in the days leading up to the war but which secured the realization of neither value in the war's aftermath, this alternative would have held out the promise of realizing both. By breaking Baathist power decisively, it would have prepared the way for a new beginning in Iraqi political life. The repression and fear that had governed the lives of Iraqis for a generation would be swept away; in its place we would have sought to erect the foundations of a civil society, largely demilitarized, whose governments came to power through democratic elections. In critical respects, this program conformed to the manifesto of the Iraqi opposition, with whom American officials refused to meet throughout the crisis, but whom we might have embraced.

The precedent for such a step is the occupation imposed on Germany and Japan in the aftermath of World War II, an occupation which succeeded in engrafting free institutions on political cultures that had endured the poison of totalitarian rule. There such a design had worked, and worked extraordinarily well. The precedent suggests that polities that have undergone the extremities of rule through terror may generate powerful tendencies in the opposite direction. So extensive is the apparatus of terror—and so effective in stifling opposition—that such impulses cannot normally come to life by themselves. But they exist under the surface in virtually all outside the ruling group. For the passive yet aggrieved population, the experience of terror creates a hunger for

146   law; the interminable afflictions of war deepen the craving for peace. Compared with what the country had endured for the previous decade of Baathist rule, this plan would have been seen for what it was: a humane and generous policy that allowed Iraqis to recuperate in peace. Releasing men and women from the fear of communal violence and rule through terror, it would simultaneously have given them hope.[1]

This alternative should be distinguished from that recommended by many critics in the aftermath of the Kurdish and Shi'a uprisings. With a few notable exceptions, the most prominent of which was the editorial board of the *Wall Street Journal*,[2] few critics of the administration's policy of nonintervention could bring themselves to support the forcible ouster of the regime in Baghdad. Most critics called simply for American actions to "level the killing field."[3] They advised against an American ground offensive against Baghdad. Some, such as the *New Republic*,[4] recommended partition as the best solution, an outcome that flowed logically from the support that would be given to Kurdish and Shi'a rebels. Partition, however, was not a promising course of action. Its great disadvantage was that it would not have produced a pacification; it would have encouraged the persistence of the sectarian and ethnic fighting that it ought to have been American policy to discourage. This could only be done through an occupation. Once such an occupation was accomplished, the prohibition of further reprisal and counterreprisal, save under duly constituted courts of law, ought to have been erected as a leading principle of the pacification.

The Bush administration was never seriously attracted to the policy under consideration here. The idea of an occupation of Baghdad, however temporary, filled administration officials with horror. As one official said,

> We decided early on if there was anything that could turn this into a Vietnam conflict it was going into densely populated areas and getting twelve soldiers a day killed by snipers. The main reason was that if we went in to overthrow him, how would we get out? If we set up a puppet government, how would we disentangle? That was the main question.[5]

The assumption that the United States would have confronted serious and protracted internal opposition, however, is questionable. In all likelihood, the Kurds and the Shi'a would have hailed us as liberators, as would have a substantial portion of Sunni Arabs who had come to detest Saddam Hussein for the misery and destruction he had brought upon their country. The overwhelming display of American military power would have provided the United States with time to form and recognize a provisional Iraqi government consisting of individuals committed to a broadly liberal platform (including demilitarization, representative government, and guarantees for minority rights). Though such a government would undoubtedly have been accused of being an American puppet, there are good reasons for thinking that it might have acquired considerable legitimacy. It would have enjoyed access, under UN supervision, to Iraq's oil revenues, which surely would have won it considerable support from the Iraqi people. The requirement that such a government devise a plan for a constituent assembly and hold free elections would also have contributed to its legitimacy. Under such circumstances, it is not clear why it would have been so difficult to withdraw American forces within six months to a year of the initial occupation. In committing itself to a relatively speedy withdrawal from Iraq, the United States might not have left behind a political situation entirely to its liking; it is nevertheless difficult to see how the condition of Iraq under such a scenario would have been worse, from the standpoint of either American interests or moral sensibilities, than what came to pass as a consequence of the Bush administration's policy.

Apart from the anticipated difficulties of an occupation, the second obstacle to such a plan was the diplomatic disarray it would presumably have produced among our Arab coalition partners and the broader international consensus achieved at the UN. It is doubtful, however, that these diplomatic difficulties would have constituted an insuperable obstacle to an occupation. To those who questioned our purposes, we would have said that we found it unconscionable to use force on the scale that was necessary to secure a military victory without at the same time providing the

148   basis for a pacification. We would have reminded the Europeans of what Europe was after World War II—"a rubble heap, a charnel house, a breeding ground of pestilence and hate"—and asked them whether they believed that we might, in good conscience, leave Iraq in the same state. To the Germans and the Japanese, we would have said that we intended to make the same contract with the people of Iraq that we had made with them—a contract that had allowed the defeated powers to peacefully recuperate, in civil freedom, if they would but break the sword. To the British and the French, we would have asked whether their own career of empire did not confirm the proposition that imperial powers have duties as well as rights, and whether the White Man's Burden and the *mission civilisatrice* with which they had once justified their own imperial rule were really undisguised hypocrisies, or rather serious obligations that an imperial power could avoid only at grave danger to its reputation for justice and humanity. *

---

* Such duties were not thought hypocrisies in an earlier age, even by Americans themselves. Indeed, once the United States acquired its own colonial empire as a consequence of the war with Spain in 1898, the American government recognized that it had incurred serious obligations to act for the benefit of those peoples it now ruled. The general policy regarding the treatment of Puerto Rico, Cuba, and the Philippines was set forth in a report prepared by Elihu Root, then Secretary of War. (See Elihu Root, "The Principles of Colonial Policy: Porto Rico, Cuba and the Philippines, [1899])," in *The Military and Colonial Policy of the United States: Addresses and Reports*, Robert Bacon and James Brown Scott, eds. [Cambridge, Mass.: Harvard University Press, 1916], pp. 161–76). In this report, Root spoke of "obligations correlative" to the absolute sovereignty entailed by the territorial acquisitions, which he said were "of the highest character":

> It is our unquestioned duty to make the interests of the people over whom we assert sovereignty, the first and controlling consideration in all legislation and administration which concerns them, and to give them, to the greatest possible extent, individual freedom, self-government in accordance with their capacity, just and equal laws, and opportunity for education, for profitable industry, and for development in civilization (pp. 161–62).

Secretary of War Henry Stimson made a similar observation in 1912: "Until our work in the archipelago is completed, until the Filipinos are prepared not only to preserve but to continue it, abandonment of the Philippines, under whatever guise, would be an abandonment of our responsibility to

To our traditional allies, these claims would have been irre- **149**
sistible. An American plan based on these principles would have
encountered no more resistance than that provoked by the plan we
did pursue. This is especially so if we remember the glue that held
the coalition together, which for many states was simply the
desirability of displaying solidarity with American aims in the
crisis. Within broad limits, we had the ability to shape the coalition to our own purposes. This was true even of the Soviet Union.
It is not a foregone conclusion that the Soviet Union would have
broken with the West, on which it was crucially dependent for a
way out of its economic morass, on the issue of an American
occupation of Iraq. The need for Western cooperation was, for
Gorbachev, a permanent factor in his diplomacy, and within the
ambit of that need American policy had a freedom of action that
gave it wide latitude in its choice of war aims.

The Arab coalition we raised up during the crisis would have
posed a more serious obstacle to such a plan. None of the gulf states
would have relished what might easily be denounced as a blatant
act of American imperialism. The Saudis would have objected to
any program that gave greater power to the Shi'a of Iraq's south,
which a representative democracy, even if not based on the principle of one man—one vote, would certainly have done. For Turkey,
Syria, and Iran, even an autonomous Kurdistan would have been
looked upon with alarm. In 1988, American contacts with the
Kurdish opposition had provoked a Turkish protest; in the course
of the 1991 risings, a Syrian official declared that an independent
Kurdistan would be a *casus belli* for both Syria and Turkey. It is
undeniably the case, therefore, that any plan that would have
given the Kurds and Shi'a a greater share of power would have
entailed serious complications with neighboring states.

---

the Filipino people and of the moral obligations which we have voluntarily
assumed before the world." (See Henry L. Stimson and McGeorge Bundy, *On
Active Service in Peace & War* [New York: Harper & Row, 1948], pp. 118–20.)
Whether the United States, in the course of its colonial experiment, lived up
to its obligations may be questioned; that it had incurred such obligations was,
however, generally acknowledged.

150   Whether these difficulties would have been insuperable, however, is doubtful. The opinions of the states neighboring Iraq allowed for considerable latitude in the choice of American war aims. The Saudis, the Syrians, and the Iranians wanted Saddam Hussein removed from power; they were equally interested in ensuring the elimination of the threat posed by Iraq's large conventional forces and by its ABC weapons programs. It might have been said to them that these aims could only be ensured if American and allied forces temporarily occupied the country. The United States might then have pledged that it would commit itself to avoiding the "Lebanonization" of Iraq, that it would promote autonomy but not partition, that it would withdraw its forces as soon as possible, that it would secure international guarantees for Iraq's political independence and territorial integrity, and that it would seek to make Iraq's rehabilitation and reconstruction an enterprise to be carried out under the auspices of the United Nations. Under these circumstances, it is highly doubtful that Iran, Turkey, Saudi Arabia, or Syria would have posed serious obstacles to such a plan.

★ ★ ★

It would be absurd to conclude that a policy of occupation and reconstruction would not have entailed serious risks. Once having gotten into Iraq and made ourselves responsible for the reconstruction of the state, it would have been difficult to get out. The sequence anticipated by some critics—"initial welcome, attempt to restore the authority of a 'legitimate' state, identification with one faction in a bitter internal dispute, growing resistance ('terrorism'), ignominious withdrawal"—was not altogether implausible.[6] The policy would have been based on a calculated gamble that the fear induced by the overwhelming display of American military power, together with the elation produced by Saddam's downfall, would have persisted long enough to create an indigenous and legitimate regime, to which would be speedily transferred the functions of internal police. It assumed the probability that each of the principal groups within Iraq—Sunni Arabs, Shi'a Arabs, and Sunni Kurds—would have seen the advantages of the new lease on life a temporary American occupation would have given them, and would have considered it to be in their self-interest to cooperate with the transitional arrangements imposed by the United States (or, insofar as that was possible, the United Nations). It assumed that the world community, or at least a substantial majority, would have supported us once they appreciated the logic of the American design and saw that we were determined to pursue it. It also assumed that other states would have cooperated with us in accepting the proposition that Iraq must remain one state, and that its borders would be guaranteed by the international community.

Even if these assumptions are granted the status of good probabilities, it nevertheless remains the case that an occupation would have represented an arduous commitment, and that it would have had to contend with imposing obstacles. Some coalition members might have broken with the United States over this issue. It might have been impossible to have secured the cooperation of the three principal groups within Iraq, forcing the United States into the midst of ethnic and sectarian issues it did not fully understand or know how to cope with. An occupation might have entailed a larger number of American casualties, either because Iraqi forces would have fought in defense of Baghdad or because a guerrilla opposition would have emerged. These considerations make it fully understandable why the Bush administration was reluctant to take on the burdens of a pacification. At a minimum, any such occupation would have subjected the administration to severe political censure at home if things had gone awry. But, if for the sake of argument, it is assumed that these burdens were so onerous as to make the occupation a political impossibility, it does not follow that the United States should be absolved of responsibility for the consequences its course of action entailed. It lends support, on the contrary, to a different conclusion: that if the United States was determined to fight a terribly destructive war that would generate obligations that the nation either could not or would not fulfill, then, short of pressing necessity, it ought not to have gone to war at all.

CHAPTER 1 3

The Redemption
of Vietnam

That the gulf war was marked from the outset by an insistence on drawing far-reaching lessons from the conflict is not surprising. Particularly for a nation given to view the world as this nation has done, every war must have its lessons. The lessons drawn may of course give rise to extended controversy, as they did notably after World War I and Vietnam. Indeed, the controversies these two wars provoked persisted for a generation, only to be set aside by subsequent wars. Whether the gulf war will in fact do for Vietnam what World War II did for its predecessor, remains to be seen. In the period immediately following the conflict in the gulf, the conclusion overwhelmingly subscribed to was that it would. No one gave more emphatic and unqualified support to this view than the president. In a radio address on the morrow of victory President Bush declared that "The specter of Vietnam has been buried forever in the desert sands of the Arabian peninsula." [1] In a similar though less formal vein he confided to a smaller group: "By God, we've kicked the Vietnam syndrome once and for all." [2]

The specter that had presumably been buried forever was the pervasive doubt that America could and would again effectively employ its military power in the world. By implication, that doubt had not been dispelled by the preceding administration. The Reagan administration had resorted to force in Grenada and Libya, and the pattern had been continued by the Bush administration in Panama but these were merely demonstrative uses of force, issuing in what were, after all, inglorious little victories. A sharp contrast was drawn between them and the triumph that had been achieved in the gulf. Whereas Reagan had vowed to break **153** from the constraints on the use of military power that had followed the experience in Vietnam, in practice he had accepted and adjusted to them. Bush, it appeared, had clearly and dramatically broken from these constraints. Having done so, and with such spectacular success, he had shown, in the words of the chairman of the House Foreign Affairs Committee, "that the American people are willing to go to war and to win."[3] At the same time, a break as effective and decisive as that represented by the gulf war was also taken to mean that in the future American power would not have to be used in any but the most exceptional of circumstances. In his first news conference following the war, the president voiced his conviction respecting America's new credibility. Responding to the question of whether he envisioned "a new era now of using U.S. military forces around the world for different conflicts that arise?" President Bush declared:

> No, I think because of what's happened we won't have to use U.S. forces around the world. I think when we say something that is objectively correct—like don't take over a neighbor or you're going to bear some responsibility—people are going to listen. Because I think out of all this will be a new-found—let's put it this way: a reestablished credibility for the United States of America.[4]

If the endgame in the gulf has nevertheless been seen by critics to cast some doubt on this reestablished credibility, it has not been substantially tarnished in the nation's eyes. Subsequent events may suggest that the objectives of the war were not as simple and clear-cut as the administration portrayed them. They may demonstrate as well that military victory is seldom so complete as to preclude the prospect of political quagmires emerging. But these complications have not dimmed the luster of military victory. The value set on winning the war, on military victory, pure and simple, is considered independently of the political criteria by which the use of force is normally judged. In this perspective, what is decisive about the Vietnam experience was that America lost a war, just as what is decisive about the gulf experience was that America won a war. The specter of Vietnam—indeed, the Vietnam syndrome itself—was first and foremost the fear of another defeat. By con-

154   trast, the promise of the gulf is that of a future in which the nation will never again be frustrated, let alone experience defeat, in war.

If this is the principal lesson gained from the war, it is surely a familiar one. It is the lesson that nations have regularly learned from victory. It is particularly the lesson great powers appear to learn from victory in war. The persuasion in victory that a logic and necessity have been revealed which are largely independent of time and circumstance—that a pattern of success has been established which, if only faithfully pursued, will assure even a distant future—is a delusion to which many have fallen victim. That it may now claim yet another victim seems altogether likely.

What is it, after all, that the gulf war taught the nation—beyond the importance of achieving victory if one does resort to war—that will preclude future defeat, that is, another Vietnam? While the list of lessons is long, those deemed crucial for ensuring against a repetition of Vietnam are only three. They were stated with admirable brevity in the aftermath of the war by R. W. Apple, Jr.: "Never go to war before insuring domestic consensus and establishing international support. . . . Never go to war without a clear objective. . . . Take no half measures." [5] These were the things that presumably were not done in Vietnam. They were the things that presumably were done in the gulf. The radically different outcomes of the two wars testify to their validity and to the price paid for abandoning them.

While in principle the first two lessons are unexceptionable, in practice rigid adherence to them may not always prove possible. Circumstances may arise in which an administration may feel compelled to go to war before ensuring domestic consensus, just as it may feel compelled to go to war without achieving complete clarity of objective. This consideration apart, however, the gulf experience, juxtaposed with Vietnam, scarcely bears out these lessons. In the case of the gulf, the president went to war before he ensured a domestic consensus. (By contrast, he did achieve remarkable international support.) He did so of necessity, moreover, since a domestic consensus was above all dependent upon the costs of the war; but the costs were largely speculative prior to the initiation of hostilities. Had the costs been substantially greater than they proved to be, and had they become apparent in the early stages of the war, the division that marked the public's outlook until the eve of hostilities might have persisted and even worsened. In the case of Vietnam an administration went to war enjoying a sturdy domestic consensus. That much-vaunted cold war consensus—a far sturdier construct than any the nation has since known—fell apart, in the main, because of the war's increasing costs and, of course, its duration. The lesson, then, is not so much that an administration should never go to war before ensuring domestic consensus as it is that the costs of war must be kept very modest if domestic consensus is to be ensured.

The second lesson of the gulf war, again as juxtaposed with Vietnam, is no less imperfectly read than the first. The clarity of objectives seen to characterize the recent conflict is as overdrawn as the lack of clarity now seen in the earlier conflict. In the case of Vietnam, American intervention was justified from the start in terms of the freedom and self-determination of South Vietnam. "Our objective," President Lyndon Johnson declared in his first major address following the initiation of aerial bombardment against North Vietnam, "is the independence of South Vietnam, and its freedom from attack. We want nothing for ourselves—only that the people of South Vietnam be allowed to guide their own country in their own way." [6] The clarity of this objective does not suffer by comparison with its equivalent in the case of the gulf: to restore the independence of Kuwait, and its freedom from Iraq's aggression. In this respect, the contrast between the two conflicts was less the clarity in stated objective supposedly marking the one (the Persian Gulf) yet not the other (Vietnam), as it was the utter disparity in the circumstances in which the two wars were fought. If this is so, then the relevant lesson of the two wars is not the need for clarity of objective but the need for favorable circumstances. Clearly, the circumstances attending the war in Vietnam were as unfavorable as those attending the war in the gulf were favorable. Unfortunately, it is not always possible to fight wars in circumstances as favorable as they were in the gulf.

It may be argued that in Vietnam it was not so much the defense of South Vietnam that testified to a lack of clarity in

156   objective as it was the larger purposes held to justify American intervention. In the address cited above, President Johnson articulated the larger purposes:

> We fight because we must fight if we are to live in a world where every country can shape its own destiny. And only in such a world will our own freedom be finally secure . . . We are also there to strengthen world order . . . To leave Vietnam to its fate would shake the confidence . . . in the value of the American commitment, the value of America's word. The result would be increased unrest and instability, and even wider war.[7]

If Kuwait is substituted for Vietnam the same words might have been employed by President Bush in articulating America's larger purpose in the gulf. In terms of the clarity of these larger objectives, there is no apparent reason to prefer one over the other.

The link drawn in the gulf between the liberation of Kuwait and world order is no clearer than the link drawn in Vietnam between preserving the independence of South Vietnam and world order; in both cases, the greater objective has been difficult to establish. As between the two, however, it may at least be said that the persuasiveness of the connection made between world order and American security was considerably greater in Vietnam than it was in the gulf. Vietnam did indeed have a larger setting, one which could plausibly be equated with international order and, in turn, the nation's core security interests. The significance Vietnam represented by 1965 was in large part the inevitable outcome of the hegemonial conflict with both the Soviet Union and China, a conflict in which each disputed interest was seen on all sides as a symbol of the whole conflict, and in which each confrontation, whether direct or indirect, was looked upon by adversaries as a test case. The gulf did not have this larger setting; given the end of the cold war, the radical decline of Soviet power and influence, and the dominance of American military power in the world, it *was* largely the setting in terms of American security interests.

Nor is this all. Whereas in Vietnam there were no unavowed objectives for which the war was fought, in the gulf there were. However insistent the Bush administration was in proclaiming its objective as being neither more nor less than the liberation of Kuwait, this was not its only objective and it may well be that it was not even its primary objective. Beyond Kuwait's liberation, **157** the administration was intent on destroying Iraq's strategic weapons, severely reducing its industrial infrastructure and, above all, effecting a change in Baghdad's government. At the same time, these objectives were not to be achieved either through the occupation of Iraq or at the price of Iraq's territorial integrity. The course of events subsequent to the war has laid bare the administration's difficulty in reconciling its unavowed objectives in going to war with the constraints on the means it was willing to employ in pursuit of those objectives, just as it has shown the conflicts that may arise between the objectives themselves. The clarity of objective the war supposedly exemplified has thus been considerably dimmed.

There remains the lesson that once in war no half measures should be taken. A military analyst has described this lesson as one reflecting a new civil-military relationship:

> This unwritten bargain said the military would never again willingly fight a major war if it did not have full political support, if it could not use all its force to win quickly and decisively, if gradual escalation and political bargaining deprived it of the ability to maintain momentum and if politicians tried micro-management." [8]

It was reliably reported that in the early stages of the gulf crisis a pledge that substantially reflected these terms was extracted from the president by the Chairman of the Joint Chiefs of Staff, General Colin Powell. In an interview given some two months before the outbreak of the gulf war, the president's senior commander in the field, General H. Norman Schwarzkopf, declared: "I can assure you that if we have to go to war, I am going to use every single thing that is available to me to bring as much destruction to the Iraqi forces as rapidly as I possibly can in the hopes of winning victory as quickly as possible." [9]

In the manner of the preceding lessons, this lesson too must be seen against the experience of Vietnam. A once revisionist view, subscribed to only by the Right and the military, has now become almost the conventional wisdom. It holds that defeat in Vietnam was largely self-imposed by a government that was as unwilling to sanction the military measures required for victory as it was insistent upon exercising a rigid control over military operations. The refusal in Vietnam to allow war to follow its own logic,

158   as determined by those versed in this logic, led inexorably to
defeat, just as the willingness in the gulf to submit to war's logic led
inexorably to victory.

The current popularity of this view notwithstanding, the
question remains: what if the political objectives sought through
war require constraints on the conduct of war? The constraints
placed by the government on the conduct of the war in Vietnam
cannot be explained simply by a misguided infatuation with theo-
ries of escalation or by a president and secretary of defense whose
personalities virtually compelled them to seek control over all
activities within their reach. While these factors are indeed significant in accounting for the way in which the war unfolded, they do
not cover the entire ground by any means. Of equal, if not greater,
significance is the broader international setting in which the
Vietnam war was fought. That setting appeared to dictate constraint if a wider war with China, and even perhaps with the
Soviet Union, was not to be risked. The sanctuaries from which
North Vietnam marshaled the resupply and reinforcement of its
troops and the ports in which Hanoi received a constant stream of
shipping from the Soviet bloc were left alone for years because of
the fear of a wider war. When in the Nixon administration that
fear markedly diminished because of the growing rapprochement
with China and the emerging détente with the Soviet Union,
what had earlier been off limits to American military forces was no
longer so.

To the larger setting that appeared to dictate constraint in
the war's conduct must be added the Vietnamese setting. The
abandonment of "half measures" against the North meant taking
measures that would have unavoidably killed large numbers of the
civilian population. The reluctance of the Johnson administration
to take such measures may be seen in retrospect as misguided, not
only in terms of military logic but in political-moral terms as well.
If so, it may only bear out the warning voiced years ago by an acute
observer: "Of all the illusions a people can cherish, the most
extravagant and illogical is the supposition that, along with the
progressive degradation of its standards of conduct, there is to go a
progressive increase in respect for law and morality." [10]

The response may be made to these considerations that, even if they are once conceded, they only show that we should have never intervened in Vietnam. Wars that can only be fought by half measures, this argument runs, should never be entered into because they may not, and likely will not, issue in complete victory. The lesson that half measures should never be taken is not merely a prescription for complete victory, it is a warning against engaging in wars that may fall short of complete victory. If you cannot be entirely successful, Secretary of Defense Dick Cheney was alleged to have counseled prior to the gulf war, don't fight. This is a luxurious view, appropriate only to a power that feels it can pick and choose its wars at convenience and that it can do so because— whether admitting this or not—such wars are not really found to respond to necessity. Where vital interests are not at stake, it makes eminent sense to engage only in wars that hold out the promise of a complete and swift victory at modest cost.

The gulf war provided an ideal setting for demonstrating this lesson. In the gulf we could do what we wanted without fear. With the cold war over and the Soviet Union a virtual supplicant, no prospect of a wider war followed from our actions. With an adversary possessed of arms no match for our own, there was no prospect of meaningful reprisal for the measures we might take. And with the political and military leadership of the nation in almost complete accord over both the objectives and conduct of the war, there was no bureaucratic obstacle to a war that spurned half measures.

These were very favorable circumstances. Yet they are the basis for a lesson that presumably rises above and is independent of circumstance. Can the lesson stand? Only if future wars resemble the gulf war in having equally favorable circumstances. If they do not, the lesson that half measures should never be taken may well prove disastrous. The real meaning of that lesson is that war is an instrument of policy only until the moment it is entered into. Thereafter it must follow a logic of its own, a logic in which all must be subordinated to complete military victory. This in turn implies that government must effectively relinquish control over war's conduct in the name and for the sake of such victory. Taken seriously, this course would represent a reversion of what we had come to look upon as the normal order of affairs.

CHAPTER 14

The Faustian Bargain

The Iraqi invasion of Kuwait presented the United States with three basic alternatives. The essence of the first strategy was the military containment of Iraq, together with punitive economic sanctions. The imperative of the second strategy was Iraq's rollback from Kuwait, together with the destruction of its armed forces for aggressive purposes but leaving it with the capability to maintain internal order. The objective of the third strategy was the dismantling of Iraqi power and the reconstruction of the Iraqi state on democratic principles. The strategy of containment rested on an appeal to American security and the regional balance of power; the strategy of rollback, while invoking these two considerations, rested preeminently on the appeal to the principle of state sovereignty and to the valuable lesson conveyed by the swift punishment of aggression; and the strategy of war and reconstruction rested preeminently on the desirability, if war were chosen, of avoiding widespread anarchy and suffering in the war's aftermath.

The argument made here is that it was not necessary to go to war to vindicate American interests in world order, regional security, and the global economy, but having gone to war, the United States ought to have pursued a strategy that broke Baathist power decisively and created the conditions for the reconstruction and rehabilitation of the Iraqi state. Even the sympathetic reader is likely to object that the argument is too clever by half, that it succeeds in indicting the Bush administration's conduct only at the price of a fatal inconsistency, and that even if assent is given to one of these alternatives it is impossible to simultaneously give **161** credence to both.

Yet the two alternatives are not as inconsistent as they may appear. The principal assumptions that they share are that the United States enjoyed overwhelming military superiority over Iraq, that such superiority gave us the freedom to remain at peace or go to war, and that the diplomatic coalition was malleable and might have been shaped in the direction we chose. We might have enlisted the international community in a protracted struggle with Iraq based on military containment and punitive economic sanctions; equally, we might have occupied the country and pursued a far more ambitious strategy without encountering insuperable obstacles from states whose cooperation was desirable (even if not, at all events, indispensable).

This freedom of action was made possible by two great events. One was the Iraqi invasion of Kuwait, which provided the *entrée* for substantial American forces in the gulf (whether defensive or offensive) while producing a solid consensus within the international community against the aggression; the other was the end of the cold war, which made it possible to act without fear of retaliation by our historic adversary but which still left us with a large number of allies willing to follow the lead marked out by the United States.

Even for an insular power whose historic experience was one of relative freedom from external constraint, this position was highly unusual. It presented a choice of fundamental historical significance. This was so not only because the choice made might well be indicative of the future pattern of American conduct. Though it is unlikely that the specific circumstances attending the conflict—Iraq's overwhelming dependence on oil exports, the absence of serious antagonism among the great and nearly great powers of the international system, the peculiar operational circumstances confronting the contending military forces, the unique circumstances of the exorbitantly wealthy yet militarily impotent Kuwaiti state—will be duplicated elsewhere, America's conduct revealed a propensity that might well find expression in different circumstances. The freedom of action the United States

162   enjoyed made what we wanted, as opposed to what external circumstances necessitated, of crucial significance. It created a powerful light that penetrated the innermost recesses of the nation's being.

What that light reveals is not a pleasant sight, for it finds the nation in the grip of a pathology. The essence of that pathology consists of the attitude now taken toward the use of force. We have fastened upon a formula for going to war—in which American casualties are minimized and protracted engagements are avoided—that requires the massive use of American firepower and a speedy withdrawal from the scenes of destruction. The formula is a very popular one, but it is not for that reason to be approved. Its peculiar vice is that it enables us to go to war with far greater precipitancy than we otherwise might while simultaneously allowing us to walk away from the ruin we create without feeling a commensurate sense of responsibility. It creates an anarchy and calls it peace. In the name of order, it wreaks havoc. It allows us to assume an imperial role without discharging the classic duties of imperial rule.

This is no formula of responsible statecraft. It offends the classic teaching that "the purpose of all war is peace." It reflects, in a profound and inescapable sense, a Faustian bargain—a contract with the devil in which the means by which war is made more palatable to us have the inescapable concomitant of increasing the misery inflicted on others. It is a bargain we enter into at grave risk to the nation's reputation for justice and humanity.

PART THREE

American Security and the National Purpose

CHAPTER 15

The Original Understanding

T he new world order articulated by President Bush builds on a set of precedents that was only established in the United States during the cold war. The assumption that the security of the United States is closely linked with the preservation of world order attracted substantial domestic support only in the course of the hegemonial contest with the Soviet Union. Even then it was supported by what may be termed a negative consensus, one that existed so long as the price attached to the nation's promissory notes was not excessive. The notion that America required sizable interventionary forces to contend with would-be aggressors throughout the world is also an idea of relatively recent vintage. Seen across a broader time frame, the development of global commitments and the heavy emphasis on military power are unusual in American history. The growth of the nation's power has given it pretensions it once shunned and provided it with temptations it seldom had to face in the past.

American diplomacy was once based upon principles very different from those prevailing today. Ironically, however, those principles now seem to be forgotten. At the very least, they are regarded as having little relevance to a nation that now stands at the center of the international system and sees itself as the world's only superpower. This state of affairs is ironic for two reasons. It was the global challenge provided by the Soviet Union that led the nation to break from many of the principles that had traditionally guided its foreign policy and to build up, in peacetime, the formidable armed forces and institutional structures of the national

166   security state. It might be thought that the disintegration of the
Soviet Union and the end of the military threat it once posed
would have led to a more critical examination of the need for
institutions and forces brought into being because of circumstances that no longer exist.

The second and greater irony is that the very factors that led
to the breakup of the Soviet Union—the failure of the communist
command economy and the unnatural suppression of democratic
yearnings throughout the Soviet empire—have often been attributed to the power of the ideas that launched the American
experiment. What Adam Smith called the "system of natural
liberty," together with the system of representative democracy
pioneered by the Founding Fathers, are seen today to represent
the truth in matters economic and political. While these two parts
of the founders' legacy are embraced wholeheartedly, other parts of
their legacy are looked upon with disdain, insofar as they are
remembered at all.

These considerations suggest the need to go back to the
beginning of the nation's history, and to give renewed attention to
the role that foreign policy was intended to play in the nation's life.
This role was closely connected with, indeed inseparable from, the
founders' conception of the nation's purpose. Their conception of
role and purpose persisted, with few exceptions, well into the
twentieth century, only to be overthrown by the exigencies of the
cold war. Such an inquiry raises three questions. First, what was
the original understanding of American security and the national
purpose, and of the role that foreign policy ought to play in
realizing security and purpose? Second, how and why did these
conceptions change in the course of the twentieth century? Third,
are any elements of that original understanding worth salvaging in
today's world?

In addressing these questions, it may be safely affirmed that
there is no going back *in toto* to the doctrines and principles that
once animated American diplomacy. The last fifty years, during
which the United States emerged as the dominant power in the
world, have altered American commitments and responsibilities
in such a way that the political separation from the rest of the
world for which Americans once yearned is no longer possible or

desirable. The growth of interdependence—whether seen in terms of the spread of novel types of military technology or in terms of the existence of a global trading and financial system that in the late eighteenth century was in its infancy—has posed new challenges for American foreign policy. It is entirely appropriate, therefore, that the legacy bequeathed by the Founding Fathers should be looked upon with a degree of skepticism, and that the point of departure for today's foreign policy must be the world as it is, not as it once was.

These considerations notwithstanding, the Founding Fathers, and those who followed them in the nineteenth century, did have a certain outlook toward military power and the role that foreign policy was to play in the life of the nation that may not be so readily dismissed. Their outlook was closely tied to their understanding of the nature of republican government, and of the purpose that America was to fulfill in both its domestic policy and its foreign policy. That outlook reflected an understanding of the factors governing the rise and fall of empires and republics that is, in fact, highly relevant today. It reflected an understanding of when and why the nation might make war that went to the core of their conception of the American purpose. If that outlook is now to be abandoned—as it was abandoned during the gulf war—it at least ought to be understood that we are doing so, and that in doing so we risk a betrayal of the distinctive purpose of the nation.

★   ★   ★

At the outset of the nation's existence, the American purpose was seen in terms of the establishment of a condition of ordered liberty. Anarchy and despotism were their polar opposites— dreaded specters from which ordered liberty would be the salvation. The national purpose was first to create the institutions under which ordered liberty could thrive, to transmit the benefits of this condition to posterity, and to extend it elsewhere in the world through the power of example.

Liberty was found to reside in written constitutions, representative governments, the protection of property, religious toleration, and the free expression of opinion. Each was considered an

168 indispensable condition of free government. Together, they promised to dry up many of the sources of discord that had led the feudal monarchies of Europe into their unending wars:

> Wars for particular dynasties, wars to support or prevent particular successions, wars to enlarge or curtail the dominions of particular crowns, wars to support or to dissolve family alliances, wars to enforce or to resist religious intolerance,—what long and bloody chapters do not these fill in the history of European politics![1]

America held out the far different prospect of being able, "by the mere influence of civil liberty and religious toleration, to dry up these outpouring fountains of blood, and to extinguish these consuming fires of war."[2] By providing for peaceful methods to transfer power, by ensuring outlets for the free expression of differences of opinion, and by removing some kinds of disputes from the political realm altogether, the founders hoped to lessen the occasions on which conflicts would arise and wars would be fought.

Most of these indispensable accompaniments of free government were well understood in the colonial period; in writing such provisions into the state constitutions formed after the Declaration of Independence, Americans were following a path marked out by those who, during the years leading up to the Revolution, had appealed to both the rights of Englishmen and the rights of man as the basis of their opposition to British policy. If sufficient latitude was given the definition of English liberty, there was very little difference between the two. Americans enjoyed ample precedents from their own experience of colonial government to construct these new institutions—the "freest of peoples had been the first to rebel."[3] But the experience of the Revolution showed that liberty was not enough. Though what were viewed as the despotic inclinations of the British crown and parliament had been overthrown, in the aftermath of the Revolution a different specter emerged, that of anarchy.

The way the Founding Fathers conceived of the problem of anarchy is of special interest today. It grew out of the fear that the league of states loosely joined by the Articles of Confederation was in danger of breaking up—a development that seemed to portend the division of the continent into rival regional confederacies.

This possibility struck many American statesmen with something **169** akin to mortal panic. For the founders, as well as for the generation that followed, the workings of the European system constituted a predicament not too dissimilar from the Hobbesian state of nature. They held up, in their minds' eyes, a sequence by which republics caught in the maelstrom of this system succumbed to war, debt, and standing armies, and whose participation in the system thereby became the primordial cause of their corruption.

Their remedy to the predicament was twofold: it lay in the establishment of a republican empire in North America and in political isolation from Europe. The one would contain the centrifugal forces that threatened to produce in America the system of interstate rivalry that had been the undoing of Europe, while also ensuring internal autonomy for the members of the Union; the other would ensure that the republican empire thus created would be as much as possible immune to corruption and decay. The establishment of representative institutions and courts to resolve disputes according to a written constitution, it was hoped, would make Americans appeal to law and not to force. That appeal—so different from the recourse to force that was the first instinct of the European powers—constituted the essence of the *novus ordo seclorum* they sought to establish.

Underlying this outlook was a profound conviction that force had a logic that was ultimately inimical to liberty. Though most Americans came to understand that "the last logic of kings is also our last logic," primary emphasis was placed on the dangers that force would entail. Jeffersonians saw in past history a dynamic by which force begot the expansion of an executive or consolidated power inevitably hostile to liberty. It had been the ruin of free states, producing Caesars, Cromwells, and Bonapartes. It was, as Madison held, "the true nurse of executive aggrandizement."

> In war, a physical force is to be created; and it is the executive will, which is to direct it. In war, the public treasuries are to be unlocked; and it is the executive hand which is to dispense them. In war, the honours and emoluments of office are to be multiplied; and it is the executive patronage under which they are to be enjoyed. It is in war, finally, that laurels are to be gathered; and it is the executive brow they are to encircle. The strongest passions and most dangerous weaknesses of the human breast; ambition, avarice, vanity, the

honourable or venial love of fame, are all in conspiracy against the desire and duty of peace.[4]

The danger that war posed to liberty lay behind Madison's conviction that a central purpose of America was to seek "by appeals to reason and by its liberal examples to infuse into the law which governs the civilized world a spirit which may diminish the frequency or circumscribe the calamities of war, and meliorate the social and beneficent relations of peace."[5] Though he believed that most projects of "perpetual peace" did honor to the hearts, but not the heads, of their authors, he nevertheless thought it worthwhile to erect as a basic rule of policy for republics that wars should be declared by the authority of the people's representatives and that they be financed out of current expenditures. "Were a nation to impose such restraints on itself, avarice would be sure to calculate the expenses of ambition; in the equipoise of these passions, reason would be free to decide for the public good."[*]

---

[*] See "Universal Peace," Hunt, ed., *Writings of Madison*, VI, 88–91. Madison's assumption that the ability to run into debt would constitute a temptation to go to war was drawn from Adam Smith's *An Inquiry into the Nature and Causes of the Wealth of Nations* (New York: Modern Library, 1937 [1776]). In that work, Smith had argued that "were the expence of war to be defrayed always by a revenue raised within the year," wars "would in general be more speedily concluded, and less wantonly undertaken" (p. 878). Because of the ability to borrow, "In great empires the people who live in the capital, and in the provinces remote from the scene of action, feel, many of them, scarce any inconveniency from the war; but enjoy, at their ease, the amusement of reading in the newspapers the exploits of their own fleets and armies" (p. 872). Smith's assumption that the accumulation of public debt "has gradually enfeebled every state which has adopted it" (p. 881), and would, in fact, ruin the nations of Europe was widely shared in America. With Smith, the Jeffersonian Republicans considered debt not only as ruinous to future generations but also as constituting a powerful temptation to go to war. Alexander Hamilton took a somewhat different view of the question, holding "not that funding systems produce wars, expenses, and debts, but that the ambition, avarice, revenge, and injustice of man produce them." ("Defense of the Funding System," *The Papers of Alexander Hamilton*, Harold Syrett et al., eds. [New York: Columbia University, 1961–79, 26 vols.], XIX, 56.) Even so, Hamilton did believe that the progressive accumulation of debt was "the natural disease of all governments." It reflected a propensity to "shift off the burden from the present to a future day—a propensity which may be expected to be strong in proportion as the form of a state is popular." He considered it difficult "to conceive any thing

It might be thought that this animus toward force was unique to the Republicans, and that Federalists did not share it, but such is not the case. The Republicans' great adversary, Alexander Hamilton, also saw war as a danger to be avoided save in circumstances of utmost necessity. He professed astonishment "with how much precipitance and levity nations still rush to arms against each other . . . after the experience of its having deluged the world with calamities for so many ages." Peace, he believed, was an object of great importance for America; it was not to be given up unless clearly necessary "to preserve our honor in some unequivocal point, or to avoid the sacrifice of some right or interest of material and permanent importance."[6] What distinguished the Hamiltonian from the Jeffersonian view of war was the method for avoiding it. For Hamilton, war was to be avoided not through the absence of preparedness but through the moderation of diplomatic ambition. His system was "ever to combine energy with moderation," and he sought to limit the pretensions of the United States toward foreign powers while strengthening the military and financial power of the country. If the methods of avoiding war were different, however, the animus toward war was second nature to both sides in this first great debate over American foreign policy. Jeffersonians and Hamiltonians alike sought to devise institutional bulwarks, prudential maxims, and moral barriers against the easy resort to war. Experience seemed to show only too clearly that nations and empires became corrupted at home and weakened abroad unless the easy resort to force were somehow tamed or suppressed.

For the first eighty years of the nation's existence (from the end of the War of American Independence until the Civil War), the nation's security requirements were conceived in a manner that followed the analysis of the framers of the Constitution. The great security problem facing the nation was acknowledged by all

---

more likely than this to lead to great and convulsive revolutions of empire." (Alexander Hamilton, "Second Report on the Public Credit, January 20, 1795," *Papers on Public Credit, Commerce, and Finance*, Samuel McKee, Jr., and J. Harvie Williams, eds. [Indianapolis: Bobbs-Merrill, 1957], p. 151.)

172   to be internal. The overwhelming specter, to which every generation gave voice, was that of a breakup of the Union, which carried
with it the danger of a state system in North America that would
breed wars, threaten republican government, and provide a basis
for European interference in American affairs. As long as the
union held, Americans felt increasingly confident that their geographical isolation from Europe provided them with a greater
measure of security than that enjoyed by any European state.

   If security might be achieved through the perpetuation of the
Union, so too might the country's purpose. That purpose was to
be, as Jefferson said, "a standing monument & example for the aim
& imitation of other countries."[7] It was reserved to Americans, as
Hamilton put it, "to decide the important question, whether
societies of men are really capable or not of establishing good
government from reflection and choice, or whether they are forever destined to depend for their political constitutions on acci-
dent and force."[8] It was to show, as had never been demonstrated
before, that a representative democratic republic could indeed
succeed. If it failed, as Albert Gallatin remarked, "the last hope of
the friends of mankind was lost or indefinitely postponed."[9]

   As these statements make clear, the nation's purpose or
mission was both inward and outward looking. If Americans
believed that their form of civilization was higher than the pol-
ished societies of Europe, they also thought that their purpose
imposed an obligation to adhere to the highest standards of conduct in their own internal and external policy. The reputation of
republican government was at stake. Understood in this sense, the
idea of a national purpose lent itself not only to displays of self-
righteousness but also to sober introspection. It directed a re-
proach not only against the characteristic delusions of despotic
governments but also against the potential betrayal of national
ideals by Americans themselves. African slavery and Indian removal were attacked on these grounds; so, too, were the wars with
Mexico and Spain in 1846 and 1898. In each of these instances,
the national purpose served as a standard by which the aberrant
ways of American democracy might be judged or held in check. It

provided a light, at once piercing and redemptive, into the dark **173**
side of the American experience.

Americans differed over whether the spread of free institutions to other nations was something that might be confidently expected in the future. There was always reason for hope; there were always strong grounds for pessimism. Jefferson himself reflected this ambivalence. He was "willing to hope, as long as anybody will hope with me," [10] that free institutions would peacefully establish a foothold even in the most highly fortified strongholds of despotic power, but he knew that there were profound obstacles to overcome. Of the nations of Europe, he wrote to Monroe in 1823, "All their energies are expended in the destruction of the labor, property and lives of their people." [11] A continent whose nations were doomed to never-ending rivalries and wars was one that afforded small prospects for the development of free institutions. The prospects were no better in the nations to the south that, in Jefferson's final years, were engaged in a protracted struggle to establish their independence from Spain. These peoples would succeed in that struggle, Jefferson thought, but "the dangerous enemy is within their own breasts. Ignorance and superstition will chain their minds and bodies under religious and military despotism." [12]

Such misgivings, which were widely shared in America, did not prevent Jefferson's countrymen from seeing the Wars of Spanish American Independence, or the Greek Revolution, or the Revolutions of 1848 as harbingers of a world where "the disease of liberty" would progressively infect growing numbers of peoples. "Do we deceive ourselves, or is it true that at this moment the career which this government is running, is among the most attractive objects to the civilized world?" Daniel Webster asked in 1832. "Do we deceive ourselves, or is it true that at this moment that love of liberty and that understanding of its true principles which are flying over the whole earth, as on the wings of all the winds, are really and truly of American origin?" [13]

The hope that free institutions would take root elsewhere was based preeminently on faith in the power of public opinion. Before the vast panoply of despotic power, it was thought that free

174   institutions would irresistibly gain a foothold in the hearts and minds of all mankind. Those who criticized American declarations of sympathy with oppressed nations seeking to regain their liberty as being weak and to no purpose mistook the spirit of the age. "The time has been," Webster said,

> when fleets, and armies, and subsidies, were the principal reliances even in the best cause. But, happily for mankind, a great change has taken place in this respect. Moral causes come into consideration . . . the public opinion of the civilized world is rapidly gaining an ascendancy over mere brutal force. . . . It may be silenced by military power, but it cannot be conquered. It is elastic, irrepressible, and invulnerable to the weapons of ordinary warfare.[14]

Despite the confidence of Americans that they had discovered principles of government that would allow every nation to improve its condition and to enjoy the blessings of civil liberty, they nevertheless disclaimed any intention of interfering in the internal affairs of other governments. "Our true mission is not to propagate our opinions or impose upon other countries our form of government by artifice or force, but to teach by example and show by our success, moderation, and justice, the blessings of self-government and the advantages of free institutions."[15] This was settled doctrine throughout the nineteenth century, although there were spirited debates over how exactly to apply this doctrine in particular circumstances (between, for instance, Jefferson and Hamilton in 1793, or Clay and Adams in 1821, or Webster and Randolph in 1824). Even the most ardent propagandists of republican institutions, however, disclaimed any intention to overthrow existing governments through American arms, and even the most caustic skeptics of the ability of other peoples to transplant successfully republican institutions acknowledged a duty to teach by example. America was "the well-wisher to the freedom and independence of all," but she was "the champion and vindicator only of her own."[16] The resort to arms was to be contemplated only in circumstances where other nations challenged our own rights and our own interests. The cause of international order, like the cause of freedom, was one to be secured ultimately by the progress of opinion. On both these scores, Americans believed that they had an important contribution to make, but it was a contribution that was not to endanger their own peace and neutrality.

In appealing to universal principles to justify American rights and interests, whether in politics or commerce, there was no intimation that the nation would surrender its freedom of action in foreign policy. Insofar as there was a multilateralist tradition, one founded on the belief in the necessity of cooperation among like-minded republican regimes, it found expression in the Union and in the belief that forbearance, practical good sense, and mutual accommodation were necessary virtues if the Union was to survive. With regard to all states that were not a part of the "empire of liberty," however, the nation reserved its freedom of action. The proscription of entangling alliances was held to apply not only to the states of Europe, which, as Washington said, had "a set of primary interests, which to us have none or a very remote relation," interests which would engage them "in frequent controversies, the causes of which are essentially foreign to our concerns." [17] The refusal to enter into alliances with foreign states was also marked with regard to the nations of South America, whose independence from outside interference bore more directly on the interests of the United States. When, in 1823, James Monroe warned the powers of the Holy Alliance "that we should consider any attempt on their part to extend their system to any portion of this hemisphere as dangerous to our peace and safety," [18] the President made no commitment to the security or freedom of any other state. As Richard Henry Dana noted,

> there is no intimation what the United States will do in case of European interposition, or what means it will take to prevent it. The United States have steadily refused to enter into any arrangement with the other American States for establishing a continental system on that point, or for mutual defence, or even to commit themselves in the way of pledge or promise. [19]

If we went to war it would be for our own reasons and for our own security. We would neither expect nor rely on the cooperation of other states.

In the original understanding, foreign policy was thus to play a limited role in the nation's life. Order and liberty were the ideals around which the nation's domestic life were to revolve, but they

176   were to be objectives of foreign policy only in an indirect and limited sense. This outlook reflected the conviction that an ambitious foreign policy carried the risk of war; war, in turn, was seen as the means by which the constitutional order at home might be deranged and America's peaceful purposes corrupted. Though conscious that there would be occasions in which war would constitute the only acceptable response to an external assault on American rights and interests, the decision for war was seen as a momentous one, to be reached only on grounds of manifest necessity. The real purpose of America lay elsewhere, in the perfection of her own civil society and in the hope that the sphere of ordered liberty thus established would constitute a benign example for other peoples who wished to imitate it.

CHAPTER 16

The Age of Uncertainty

With but few exceptions, the principles of nonentanglement in Europe's political affairs, neutrality in Europe's wars, and nonintervention in the internal affairs of other states characterized the outlook of American diplomatists from the nation's founding until the end of the nineteenth century. The duty to teach by example was continually reiterated, as was the American commitment to the peaceful settlement of disputes. The epoch that followed, which may be dated roughly from the Spanish-American War of 1898 to Japan's attack on Pearl Harbor in 1941, was by contrast a period of uncertainty. Under force of circumstance, and in consciousness of vastly enlarged power, intimations began to appear of a seismic shift in the permanent bases of American foreign policy. The old doctrine and the old faith began increasingly to be questioned, though it was not until World War II and the onset of the cold war that they were overturned.

The acquisition of a colonial empire, as a consequence of the war with Spain, was one sign that the traditional diplomatic principles of the nation might no longer be an adequate guide to current circumstances. In undertaking a humanitarian intervention in Cuba against the depredations of Spanish power, and in acquiring the remnants of the overseas Spanish colonial empire, the United States set sail on an uncharted sea. Never before had the nation acquired by conquest sovereignty over a large and sedentary people whom it had no intention of bringing into the Union. In fomenting rebellion in the Panamanian province of

178   Colombia, so as to bring to power a government amenable to the construction of the Panama Canal, the American government committed an equally apparent violation of the principle of nonintervention. ("Have I defended myself?" [against the charge of impropriety] Theodore Roosevelt asked his cabinet after the Panamanian intervention. "You certainly have," Elihu Root reputedly replied. "You have shown that you were accused of seduction and you have conclusively proved that you were guilty of rape." [1]) In refusing to recognize Victoriano Huerta's government in Mexico in 1913, on the ground that it had come to power by violent means, Woodrow Wilson departed from the traditional recognition policy of the U.S. government, which, in accord with the broader doctrine of nonintervention, accorded de facto recognition to any government that met the test of effectiveness.

In these instances, and in others, there was no denying that a change had taken place. Particularly in relation to the nations of the Caribbean and Central America (which, like Mexico, were too far from God and too close to the United States), the doctrine of nonintervention often came to be honored in the breach. Even the doctrine of isolation and nonentanglement came to be seen by many Americans as too confining. More and more Americans came to argue, as former secretary of state Richard Olney did in 1900,

> that the international policy suitable to our infancy and our weakness was unworthy of our maturity and our strength; that the traditional rules regulating our relations to Europe, almost a necessity of the conditions prevailing a century ago, were inapplicable to the changed conditions of the present day; and that both duty and interest required us to take our true position in the European family and to both reap all the advantages and assume all the burdens incident to that position. [2]

It was only with American participation in World War I, however, that the policy of nonentanglement in Europe's affairs was shaken in its foundations. With the outbreak of European war in 1914, indications appeared that threats to American security might arise from the wars of other continents—an idea that had been common currency during the wars of the French Revolution and Napoleon but that had been progressively forgotten during the long peace between 1815 and 1914. The proximate cause of **179** America's intervention in World War I—certainly the cause felt most deeply by public opinion—was Germany's decision to launch unrestricted submarine warfare in early 1917 and the unmistakable challenge that decision posed to American neutral rights and honor. But an articulate minority of Americans had also become increasingly fearful that a German victory would imperil either American security or republican institutions. Neo-Hamiltonians warned that a German victory would break the sea lines of communication across the Atlantic and derange the European balance of power, inevitably posing a threat to American security; neo-Jeffersonians feared that such a victory might force the United States to build armaments to counter the threat of German militarism. To a nation that had prided itself on the doctrine that its influence would spread peaceably and by example, such an outcome appeared ominous. As Wilson's advisor, Colonel House, wrote, it would "change the course of our civilization and make the United States a military nation."[3]

The contrast between the limited aim for which the United States went to war in 1917 (the protection of neutrality and the freedom of the seas) and the war aims it subsequently embraced has often been noted by historians. Though the United States entered the war as an associated power and thereby advertised the distinction between American and allied war aims, Wilson came increasingly to see the war as a crusade to make the world safe for democracy and to establish a world organization devoted to the collective realization of universal ideals. It was no narrow partisan feeling that led Senator Henry Cabot Lodge to reject Wilson's vision of collective security as a betrayal of American diplomatic traditions, of "the policy of Washington and Monroe"; yet Wilson's ideal lived on in American diplomacy in the twentieth century.

The debate between Wilson and Lodge over the League of Nations is worth recalling today, because it touched matters that went to the heart of America's purpose as a nation that was now indisputably a first-class world power. Wilson's insistence that America make a moral commitment to the "territorial integrity

180   and political independence" of all league members was undertaken in the conviction that the force of world public opinion and, if necessary, economic sanctions would assure a satisfactory result in 99 percent of the cases that might come before the League. The idea that the United States might become the policeman of the world to vindicate this principle was utterly foreign to the president's outlook. Lodge, on the other hand, rejected the notion that the United States ought to obligate itself to a solemn commitment it might be unwilling to fulfill; he saw no necessary connection between the prevention of aggression everywhere in the world and the vindication of American security. "In effect," as historian Roland Stromberg has summarized the dispute over the League, "Wilson and the Democrats wanted to accept an obligation that we might thereafter refuse, while Lodge and the Republicans wanted to refuse an obligation we might thereafter accept." [4]

Wilson, like Jefferson a century before, embraced grand objectives in the world but dismissed the need for war to accomplish them. Indeed, the whole purpose of the League of Nations, as Wilson conceived it, was to avoid the need for war. By contrast, the moderate Republicans, of whom Lodge, Root, and Roosevelt were the leaders, believed that war would remain the final arbiter among nations; they had always argued for preparedness. Like their intellectual forebear, Alexander Hamilton, they wished to confine the use of such power to objectives that had a direct relation to America's own security. They were willing to consider particular alliances with France and England to maintain the peace settlement, but thought the idea of a universal alliance against aggression to be dangerous nonsense. As Elihu Root remarked: "If it is necessary for the security of Western Europe that we go to the support of, say, France if attacked, let us agree to do that particular thing plainly. . . . I am in favor of that. But let us not wrap up such a promise in a vague universal obligation." [5]

The debate over the League, important as it was in the adumbration of themes that would remain significant for the remainder of the century, nevertheless signified no lasting change of policy. In the aftermath of the war, Americans attempted to revert, as best they could, to the original understanding of American foreign policy. They wisely rejected the indefinite commitment to the territorial integrity and political independence of other states thought to be entailed by membership in the League of Nations. Far less wisely, they came to believe that American intervention had not been necessary to avert a German victory and the dangers to security and republican institutions that such a victory would have brought. The nation reverted to its former conviction that all the European powers were animated by selfish ambitions (and as such were morally equivalent), and hence it refused the alliance with England and France that was necessary to preserve the peace settlement. American involvement in World War I was increasingly seen as an aberration, and it was thought that a reversion to America's traditional policy of no entangling alliances would pose no danger to American security. The country was secure and prosperous. Calvin Coolidge, who was a far more acute theorist of the old American order than is generally realized, summarized with his customary economy the security position of the nation in his 1926 State of the Union message: "The American people are altogether lacking in an appreciation of the tremendous good fortune that surrounds their international position," he observed. "We have no traditional enemies. We are not embarrassed over any disputed territory. We have no possessions that are coveted by others; they have none that are coveted by us. Our borders are unfortified. We fear no one; no one fears us."[6]

Coolidge's assessment assumed the permanence of an order of power that was already passing. The "tremendous good fortune" that characterized the nation's security position, and that had done so since the early nineteenth century, had been the result of circumstances that would not survive the immediate years ahead. A benign balance of power over which Great Britain had presided for a century had been put to a supreme test in World War I and had only barely survived. It had been this power balance that in part had enabled the United States to pursue a policy of hemispheric isolation. The nation's isolation had also been made possible by its geographical position. This circumstance, however, would also soon be challenged by the rapidly changing technology of war. In just over a decade, airpower would challenge the protec-

182   tion once afforded by the great ocean moats. These adverse developments would soon coincide with the rise in the 1930s of aggressive dictatorial regimes in Europe and Asia, regimes hostile to democratic societies and intent on destroying the postwar status quo. In the two continents, Germany and Japan would initiate a course of territorial conquest in pursuit of what each proclaimed to be a "new order" of the future.

It was in these changed circumstances that America abandoned its policy of isolation and eventually intervened in World War II. It did so, in the first instance, out of fear that a fascist victory would threaten the physical security of the Western Hemisphere and, ultimately, of the United States itself. A hostile power in control of Europe—or even worse, a combination of hostile powers in control of Eurasia—would possess a potential military strength superior to that of the New World. In these circumstances, it seemed quite plausible to conclude, America would become a beleaguered fortress, required to expend all of her energies in defense of the hemisphere.

The principal argument for abandoning a policy of isolation thus followed traditional balance of power considerations. In a balance of power system, as Walter Lippmann argued at the time, isolation "is the worst of all possible predicaments." [7] The logic of such a system requires allies sufficiently dependable and powerful to meet and defeat a challenge to one's security should it arise. Isolationists, Lippmann and others contended, remained blind to this fundamental truth because of their conviction that the nation's security was unconditioned by events occurring beyond the Western Hemisphere. Although this analysis of the American position eventually came to enjoy widespread acceptance, it did so only after Axis victories had put the isolationist view to the test and found it wanting. The decline and collapse of interwar isolationism came when the progress of the war appeared to hold out the prospect of an Axis victory, hence the prospect of an America alone in a hostile world. In such a world, America would be permanently confined to a defensive role in the Western Hemisphere. To forestall an imbalance of power that, it was feared, would sooner or later directly threaten the nation's security, the decision was made to adopt a policy that eventually led to intervention in the war.

CHAPTER 17

The Cold War Consensus

Substantially the same considerations led to a course of action in the wake of World War II that made the cold war inevitable. The postwar policy of containment emerged from what was perceived as a threat to American security arising from a weak and unstable Western Europe over which the Soviet Union might eventually extend its control. The initial measures of containment, the Marshall Plan and the North Atlantic Alliance, expressed the vital American interest in preserving the security and independence of the nations of Western Europe. In the context of growing Soviet-American rivalry, these measures constituted clear acknowledgment that Soviet domination of Western Europe might shift the global balance of power against the United States, thus creating a threat to America's physical security. Short of this, a Soviet-dominated Europe, it was widely assumed, would create a security problem for the United States, the solution of which would strain the nation's resources and jeopardize its institutions.

In retrospect, the dominant postwar estimate of the threat held out to America's security appears exaggerated, given the preponderance of power the nation enjoyed in those years and particularly given its sole possession of the atomic bomb. At the time, however, that estimate did not seem unreasonable. For Americans of the middle to late 1940s, the most relevant experience was World War II, an experience that included not only the threat of an Axis victory but also, between 1939 and 1941, the prospect of a Eurasia partitioned and controlled by Germany, Russia, and Japan. Even to a preponderant America, apprehen-

183

184   sion over a revival of that prospect, though with the Soviet Union as its sole architect and director, did not seem unreasonable.

A traditional conception of security, then, was the principal consideration in causing the great transformation of American foreign policy from the late 1930s to the late 1940s. It was the fear that the world balance of power might shift decisively against the United States, thereby posing a direct threat to our core security, that above all prompted the historic departure from a policy of isolation. At the same time, American security was closely tied to considerations of a more general nature. Both before and after World War II, a pressing security need was linked with a justification for repelling aggression that invoked international law (order) and with a certain diagnosis of the conditions in which peace might be secured (the spread of free institutions). Neither of these ideas would have been foreign to the outlook of the Founding Fathers, who had made the law of nations part of our supreme law and who generally believed that free institutions contributed to international peace. What was novel was the degree to which the United States was now thought obligated to assume responsibility for ensuring compliance by aggressor states with the law of nations and for establishing a protective umbrella over selected areas of the world under which free institutions would prosper.

These departures from traditional policy were accompanied by a reversal of the nation's long-standing attitude toward "entangling alliances." Having previously abjured commitments in peacetime to the security of any other state, the United States entered into the North Atlantic Treaty Organization in 1949 for the purpose of containing the expansion of the communist movement led and supported by the Soviet Union. The nation entered the compact creating this security community with a conviction that our fate was intimately tied to Europe's and with a belief in close cooperation among democratic states. Both the conviction in a common fate and the belief in cooperative action among free governments harkened back to the motives that had led to the establishment of the American union in 1787. Both dates—1787 and 1949—signified the creation of an empire of liberty.

America's new world role would have provoked far greater domestic dissension than it did—and in all probability would not have been taken up at all—were it not for the fact that the threat posed by the Soviet Union to free institutions and to international order was simultaneously a threat to American security. The threat posed by the Soviet Union could be expressed in terms of a realist concern with American security just as much as an idealist defense of legal principle or free institutions. For different reasons, Americans arrived at a common conclusion: the Soviet Union had to be contained. During the cold war, Americans debated whether containment should be particularist or universalist, and whether the primary danger stemmed from the great power threat emanating from the Soviet Union or from communism as such. Nevertheless, a rough equation was readily established between ensuring order and protecting freedom, on the one hand, and providing for security on the other. The equation united otherwise disparate outlooks and held under its capacious roof Republicans and Democrats, realists and idealists, and all varieties of the tough-minded and woolly-headed. It formed the solid foundation of the cold war consensus, which the party squabbles and partisan divisions of the day barely disturbed.

The strength of the cold war consensus explains why Americans readily consented to the establishment of institutions and governing practices they had previously identified with despotic governments. The establishment, in peacetime, of standing military forces more powerful than those of any nation on earth; the creation of intelligence agencies charged not only with assessing threats but also with conducting covert operations; the claim by the presidency of the authority to employ American military forces on short notice and without congressional consent—all this would have been looked upon by the Founding Fathers as incompatible with the maintenance at home of free institutions. Yet enemies learn one another's weapons; indeed, they must do so. For a state with the political traditions of the United States, such institutions might be justified only on the grounds of manifest necessity, as a regrettable, yet inescapable, departure from norms and practices we wished to maintain but could not. It attested to

186   the strength of the cold war consensus that not only were such
institutions and practices accepted during the classic period of the
cold war but that they even came to be seen as part of the natural
order of things.

The two great Asian land wars that occurred during this
period, Korea and Vietnam, had a profound effect on the cold war
consensus, though they did so in markedly different ways.
Whereas the Korean war solidified, if it did not create, this
consensus, the war in Vietnam badly shook, but did not break, the
same consensus. The American intervention in Korea laid the
bases of containment policy in Asia. At the time, the decision to
intervene provoked little controversy. This was partly because of
the fortuitous circumstances that permitted the United Nations
Security Council to sanction the American-led action in Korea in
the summer of 1950. Far more significant, however, was the
apparent threat to Japanese security held out by the aggression
against South Korea, if that aggression were to go unopposed. The
most important consideration was the connection drawn at the
time between Korea and Western Europe. Following the events it
did—the communist coup in Czechoslovakia, the Berlin blockade, the Soviet explosion of an atomic device, and the Chinese
communist accession to power—Korea was interpreted as part of a
mounting communist offensive which, if left unopposed, might
well eventuate in an armed attack against Western Europe. This
fear explains the relative absence of dissent to the Korean intervention and, indeed, to the other measures taken in Asia at the
time. The challenge to order represented by the North Korean
attack was thus seen as a challenge to American security, an idea
that largely neutralized early criticism of extending American
containment policy to Asia. By a similar chain of reasoning, and
despite the autocratic features of the South Korean regime, it was
also seen as a threat to free institutions.

In Korea, the elements that made up the emerging cold war
consensus not only survived the war intact but were measurably
strengthened. The criticism of the war that eventually did arise did
not challenge the security explanation for intervening but the
apparent inability of the American government either to achieve

military victory or to conclude a satisfactory agreement to end
the hostilities. By contrast, the cold war consensus was seriously
questioned a decade and a half after Korea by critics of the
Vietnam war.

The Johnson administration's insistence that the United
States was protecting South Vietnam against North Vietnamese
aggression was met by the criticism that the war in Vietnam was
above all a civil war and could not be properly classified as a case of
counterintervention (which was the only basis for the legality of
the American presence under international law). The hope that
free institutions would take root in South Vietnam came to be
regarded as a quixotic aspiration that bore little relation to Vietnamese history or to current realities. Finally, and perhaps most
crucially, the link between establishing ordered liberty in Southeast Asia and ensuring American security came to seem less and
less plausible. Because of the difficulty of making this equation,
much of the justification for continued involvement in Vietnam
came to rest on the fact, which was indisputable, that America
had staked its prestige on the outcome. At the beginning, the
justification (the equation among order, liberty, and security) had
provided the basis for the commitment. At the end, the commitment itself became the justification.

Despite the doubts and anguish that it produced, Vietnam
had a lesser effect on American foreign policy than many observers
feared (or hoped) at the time. Though a general reassessment of
American interests in the Third World occurred, particularly in
the 1970s, America's core alliances in Europe and Japan survived
intact. Nor did Americans draw the conclusion from Vietnam that
freedom was an ideal from which the nation should now turn away.
Indeed, the promotion of freedom became the centerpiece of
efforts under both Carter ("human rights") and Reagan ("the
democratic revolution") to restore the domestic consensus on
foreign policy, though the price the nation was willing to pay for
the promotion of freedom was now very modest.

The effect of Vietnam on American attitudes toward the use
of force was perhaps most problematic. One segment of domestic
opinion concluded that American blood and treasure might be

188   ventured in war only under circumstances where a direct threat to security was present. This skeptical attitude toward the use of force revived older conceptions of the circumstances under which the nation might make war. Though often labeled the "Vietnam syndrome," it in fact had much deeper roots in the nation's history. It was challenged, however, by a view which saw the failure in Vietnam not as a result of misguided ends but of incoherent means. Remarkably similar to the criticism of the "limited war" fought by Truman in Korea, the criticism of Vietnam from the political Right came to be widely regarded as one of the principal lessons of the war. Rechristened as a noble cause and as an attempt to promote freedom and ensure order, Vietnam demonstrated that the American people would support wars only if our objective was to win. Domestic support for war, on this view, rested not only on the demonstration of a link to American security; it rested equally on the adoption of a war plan in which victory was sought as rapidly as possible and through the use of overwhelming force.

CHAPTER 18

The End of the Cold War

Though defeat in Vietnam did not in the end fundamentally change the basic presuppositions of American foreign policy, it appeared to many observers that victory in the cold war might well do what defeat could not. The fundamental reorientation of Soviet foreign policy introduced by Mikhail Gorbachev, together with the breakdown of the economy in the Soviet Union, made the Soviet threat radically different. When the old guard was thrown out of office throughout the traditional Soviet *glacis* in Eastern Europe in 1989, it constituted an epochal development that forced a rethinking of the assumptions that had guided American foreign policy for nearly half a century. The end of the cold war dramatically improved the American security position. It also vindicated the American purpose, which had always been to show the peoples of the world through peaceful example that free institutions and free markets constituted the key by which their political oppression and economic misery might be lifted.

The internal disarray of the Communist powers (for the Soviet Union was not alone in suffering from the internal contradictions of communist rule) contributed to circumstances in international relations for which it is difficult to find a true parallel in the history of the modern states system that grew up in Europe in the seventeenth and eighteenth centuries and that finally encompassed the globe in the twentieth. Save for one or two unusual moments in international history (the prime example being the collaboration among the victors after the Napoleonic wars), an-

190   tagonism had always existed among the great powers at the core of
the system. For the Soviet Union to give up its empire in Eastern
Europe by default was so contrary to the normal behavior of great
powers that its verbal professions could hardly be believed until
they were acted upon.

The implications of this change for American foreign policy
were highly paradoxical. The novel situation that came to exist in
relations between the superpowers made the cold war connection
between world order and American security more tenuous than
ever. Without a great power base behind them, the threat posed to
American security by what minor despots remained was sharply
diminished. At the same time, the enhanced cooperation between the superpowers made it possible for the United States to
entertain objectives in the world (particularly on the periphery)
that had previously been stymied by antagonism at the center.

The favorable circumstances in international relations that
allowed the United States to entertain a renewed vision of world
order also made it less necessary to do so for purposes of security.
These circumstances broke the equation that had been established
during the cold war among freedom, order, and security. The
nation's freedom to turn inward and to devote attention to domestic purposes was greater than it had been since the 1920s; but, by
virtue of the same development, it also had a greater temptation
than ever before to pursue the role of leader on behalf of world
order.

It was under these circumstances that the Bush administration confronted Iraq's aggression against Kuwait. The most striking feature of its response was the insistence that the equation
among order, freedom, and security still held. It attempted to
restore the cold war consensus absent the cold war and the threat
of communism. It did so through its insistence that aggression
anywhere in the world, if not repelled, constituted a threat that
would ultimately endanger not only world order and free institutions but also American security—thus closely identifying disorder in the world with threats to American security. It did so
through its insistence that the president has the authority to go to
war, even on a massive scale, without seeking congressional autho-

rization—a claim that was made for the first time in American history in the aftermath of World War II. It did so, more generally, in its claim that the world remained a dangerous place, which required the United States to maintain powerful (even if reduced) interventionary forces to contend with would-be aggressors.

The role of America in the new world order represents a marriage of two opposing traditions in American foreign policy, without the limitations that were characteristic of either. The tradition represented by Jefferson and Wilson entertained grand ambitions in the world but was equally insistent on achieving these ambitions through measures short of war. The tradition represented by Hamilton and Lodge eschewed grand ambitions and insisted that foreign policy be tied to the pursuit of limited national interests, while at the same time it saw the need for military preparedness and believed that military force would remain the great arbiter of conflicts among nations. Bush's vision of foreign policy embraces universal aspirations and military force. It is an authentic offspring of both traditions, but one from which each parent would have recoiled. It offends the Hamilton-Lodge tradition by virtue of its universalism; it offends the Jefferson-Wilson tradition by virtue of its reliance on force. A product of the past half century, Bush's vision combines the outlook and institutions necessitated by a global challenge to the nation's security and purpose with circumstances altogether different from those which justified the initial response.

CHAPTER 19

Paradoxes of the Gulf War

I f uncertainty persists about the meaning of the new world order, it is largely because the war that was fought in its name was marked throughout by paradox and ambiguity. This was so in at least four vital respects.

1. From the beginning of the gulf crisis, the president associated the new world order with the principle that aggression against the territorial integrity of other states would not be allowed to stand. At the same time, however, the administration clearly placed great weight on the need to destroy Iraq's military machine, including its incipient capabilities in weapons of mass destruction. This barely disguised motive for the war recalled the classic justification for preventive war, which has always been that offensive war is an indispensable and justified means for dealing with future, though probable, threats to the vital interests of a state. The acceptance of this logic by the Bush administration represents a break not only from the original understanding of American diplomacy but also from the position consistently taken by American administrations since the outset of the cold war. It also departs from settled principles of contemporary international law. The condemnation of preventive (as distinguished from preemptive) war is clear and follows from the twentieth century movement to restrict the occasions on which states may lawfully resort to force. Heretofore, the United States has been a consistent supporter of this movement. From the vantage point of its hegemonial military position, however, it now appears tempted to dispense with the rules when the latter prove inconvenient.

2. A similar ambivalence characterized the American effort   **193**
to achieve a consensus at the United Nations. Despite the emphasis the administration placed on multilateral support, it was
clear from the beginning that the whole sustained effort would not
have been carried through without the iron determination of the
president to achieve his objective. That determination, however,
would not have suffered frustration; in the wake of the war,
President Bush acknowledged that he would not have acted differently had he faced insurmountable opposition at the UN. Apart
from Great Britain, which saw eye to eye with the United States
throughout the crisis, and the Arab coalition states of Saudi
Arabia, Egypt, and Syria, who wished along with Israel to see
Saddam Hussein destroyed, many other states (the Soviet Union,
China, Japan, France, Iran, India, and even Germany) had serious reservations about the course chosen by the United States.
Their doubts were ignored in Washington and their protests, such
as they were, were ineffectual. Perhaps the most impressive feature
of the gulf war is not that other states entertained these doubts but
that they were either unwilling or unable to deflect the course
chosen by the president. The recurrence of this quite remarkable
circumstance clearly cannot be relied upon in future crises. When
it cannot, is it reasonable to assume that American power will be
constrained or that an American president will act, as Mr. Bush
asserted he would have acted, unilaterally? If the gulf crisis sup-
ports the latter assumption, the crisis may herald, despite all
outward appearance, an era of American unilateralism.

3. The Janus-faced character of the new world order was
equally marked with regard to the conduct of the war that was
fought in its name. The president insisted that he had no quarrel
with the people of Iraq, and that American military forces would
take extraordinary measures to avoid the direct targeting of the
civilian population. He contrasted the superior morality of the
American war plan with the obscene tactics Iraq employed in
using Scud missiles against Israel and Saudi Arabia. At the same
time, the indirect effects of the American bombing on Iraq's
civilian population were devastating, largely because the administration defined its military objectives so broadly as to include the
whole infrastructure of modern services that supported civilian life

194   in the country. The president's invocation of the just war tradition did not prevent the waging of a war the consequences of which show that the circumstances in which war remains an "apt and appropriate" and, accordingly, a just means have further narrowed, particularly given the conditions the nation has imposed upon the wars it will wage.

4. Finally, though both order and liberty were invoked by the administration in the days leading up to the war, neither order nor liberty was established in Iraq in its aftermath. The Shi'a and Kurdish peoples within Iraq, who mistook the president's call to overthrow Saddam Hussein as a pledge of support and protection and who rose up in response, were then left alone to suffer the might of Saddam Hussein's fury.

In the gulf war, then, the United States invoked international law but was impatient with the restraints that it imposed; it postulated the need for multilateral support but was willing to act apart from an international consensus; it declared its adherence to the restraints of *jus in bello* but sorely tested the limits of those constraints in its actual conduct of the war; and it avowed its fidelity to order but was unwilling to assume the responsibility, as imperial powers have normally done, of actually imposing order in the aftermath of the war.

Seen from the philosophical perspective of the Founding Fathers, this pattern of conduct can hardly be considered surprising. Their guiding assumption was that power, unless checked and balanced, would fill whatever vacuums it could; the dominant fact about the gulf crisis was that checks that had previously restrained American power were weak and unavailing. The United States faced an adversary over which it enjoyed decisive military superiority. It had built up a powerful military machine in the course of its rivalry with the Soviet Union. The historic adversaries against which this force had previously been arrayed were in retreat, broken by internal discord and incapable, by virtue of their dependence on the West, of offering resistance to American plans. Laurels would be gathered in a victorious war, and it was the executive brow they would encircle. With so many factors in conspiracy against the desire and duty of peace, it can hardly occasion surprise that the president found it expedient to go to war.

Given the permissiveness of the international environment, what the United States wanted, as opposed to what external necessities dictated, was of crucial significance in determining the pattern of American conduct. Domestic considerations therefore inevitably came to the fore. That war was chosen despite the strength of the forces boxing in Saddam Hussein was owing above all to these domestic pressures. The administration, fearing Carterization, viewed the prospect of a protracted engagement with Saddam Hussein with alarm. The American people had never been happy with the policy of containment, even when applied to the Soviet Union. That policy ill-fitted the national character, as its critics so often pointed out. If containment was accepted during the cold war, it was largely because the alternatives (often characterized as suicide or surrender) appeared so dangerous. There was, however, an alternative in this case. A deeply rooted public impatience with a strategy of long-term containment accounts for the readiness with which the United States went to war against Iraq in the first place; the fear of American casualties accounts for the extraordinarily destructive character of the ensuing conflict. These two fears were also of critical importance in the decision to stop short in American war aims and to refuse (behind the shield of a disfigured doctrine of "nonintervention") the arduous burdens of a pacification. They say a great deal about us as a nation in terms of the kind of foreign policy we can pursue.

That the United States undertook an imperial role without discharging the classic duties of imperial rule reflected an extraordinary disjunction between power and responsibility. This disjunction alone must cast grave doubt on the proposition that the American nation is really well-suited for its new calling as the primary military enforcer of the new world order. The difficulty is not that our purpose of ordered liberty can never be effectively pursued through the use of force; the experience of the successful occupation imposed upon Germany and Japan in the aftermath of World War II demonstrates otherwise. But unless war is the only way to defend truly vital interests—as it was in World War II but

196   was not in the gulf war—it is unlikely that we will be willing to complete the circle and accept the responsibilities that the use of force imposes on us. Faced with the domestic constraints that were so apparent in the gulf war, an imperial power whose central *raison d'être* is the maintenance of order may nevertheless act as an agent of disorder. A nation whose central purpose was once the protection of ordered liberty thus acts today to achieve neither when it resorts to arms.

It will be said, in response to these considerations, that the gulf war was *sui generis* and that we are in no danger of repeating the experience. Only in the gulf, it might be said, do there exist the vital interests that might animate an ideology of world order that will otherwise remain lifeless. The American people, according to this view, are increasingly preoccupied with their domestic affairs and wish for nothing better than to be relieved of the burdens and responsibilities of world leadership. U.S. military interventions, it might be added, will probably require the political and financial support of allied states, a condition for global activism that will serve as a standing check on the willingness of a president so disposed to conduct military interventions.

That these restraining factors exist is clear; their weight, however, is not. Counterbalancing them is an equally impressive set of factors which, considered together, make up the imperial temptation. The United States is now the world's preeminent military power, with a global reach far surpassing that of any great empire in the past; it went to war on the avowed basis of a doctrine which held that aggression anywhere in the world constituted a threat to international order that it was the duty of the United States to repel, and on the unavowed basis that the threats posed by even small states, if they seek to acquire weapons of mass destruction, must be nipped in the bud before they do so. Its way of war was enormously popular at home, allowing the American people to insulate itself from the suffering normally attendant on war while rescuing the president from a position at home that had become increasingly vulnerable to attack. If the highly unusual circumstances that now prevail in international society—which make both former adversaries and traditional allies either unable or unwilling to oppose us—are added to these factors, it hardly seems excessive to warn that the United States may again face powerful temptations to repeat the experience of the gulf.* The gulf war has shown that isolationist sentiments among the public, expressed above all in their desire to avoid casualties to American troops and to avoid protracted engagements, may nevertheless be combined with an interventionist disposition to produce an explosive mixture—one marked both by the desire to employ massive force and the wish to disengage from the scenes of destruction. The gulf war was not the first manifestation of that tendency; the Panamanian intervention in 1989, though on a much smaller scale, revealed many of the same characteristics.

At bottom, the belief that the United States will not give in to the imperial temptation rests on the belief that we are different, that American power will not be misused, that we are exempt from the weaknesses and imperfections of human nature. The cruel and bitter irony is that, in thus celebrating our exceptionalism, we have forgotten some of the very elements of our political order that were intended to make us exceptional. Those elements consist of limits on the circumstances in which we might make war and self-imposed restrictions on the fulfillment of our mission that are now regarded as feeble and unbecoming the conduct of the world's preeminent military power.

---

* The warning of a great conservative, Edmund Burke, may be recalled: "Among precautions against ambition, it may not be amiss to take one precaution against our *own*. I must fairly say, I dread our *own* power and our *own* ambition; I dread our being too much dreaded." Burke added: "It is ridiculous to say we are not men, and that, as men, we shall never wish to aggrandize ourselves in some way or other . . . we may say that we shall not abuse this astonishing and hitherto unheard of power. But every other nation will think we shall abuse it. It is impossible but that, sooner or later, this state of things must produce a combination against us which may end in our ruin." ("Remarks on the Policy of the Allies with Respect to France," *The Works of Edmund Burke*, 12 vols., [Boston: Little, Brown, and Company, 1901] IV, 457.)

CHAPTER 20

Renovation

Writing in the midst of the Mexican War, and on the occasion of the death of John Quincy Adams, William Seward argued that "All nations must perpetually renovate their virtues and their constitutions, or perish." Never, Seward added, "was there more need to renovate ours than now, when we seem to be passing from the safe old policy of peace and moderation into a career of conquest and martial renown."[1] Seward's emphasis on "renovation," by which he meant the return to, and renewal of, first principles, was a theme continually articulated by the generation of statesmen who succeeded the Founding Fathers. The theme was in fact much older, being an essential element of the classical republican tradition from which the founders themselves drew so much of their own thought. It assumed that every republic stood in danger of a corruption in which public virtue was lost and purpose was betrayed. There were, and are, many variations on this theme. In the late eighteenth century, some of the most important agencies of this corruption were thought to be a burdensome public debt, overweening executive power, and standing military forces—phenomena, it was thought, that were both the cause and consequence of war.

The founders of the American state, it may be thought, ought to exercise no special hold on our outlook; the earth, as Jefferson said, belongs to the living. At the least, however, it is sobering to reflect that the nation has assumed many of the very traits that it was founded to escape. It enjoys the possession of military forces of far greater reach and power than any empire known to history. Its president lays claim to the authority not only **199** to dispatch American military forces wherever he wishes in the world but to commit them to war on his own authority. It has contracted the habit of taxing the future to pay for its present needs, so much so, indeed, that at the present time the gap between its revenues and expenditures is larger than what it spends on a military establishment that is superior to any on earth.

It is true that this formidable colossus of power was brought into being for the best of reasons. The old policy of isolation from Europe had reached a dead end in the 1930s, both in its commercial and political aspects. The Smoot-Hawley tariff of 1930, together with the neutrality legislation later in the decade, represented the hypertrophy of the old isolationist tradition in circumstances that justified its partial abandonment. Before the hostility and strength of the totalitarian great powers, the traditional emphasis on the power of example appeared as a cruel delusion; before that hostility and strength, American security was placed in serious danger. America abandoned isolationism not simply because a fascist victory was thought to threaten the nation's physical security. A fascist victory was also seen to threaten the nation's historic purpose, since such victory carried the prospect of a world in which American ideas of international order and, of course, American institutions would be rejected. In this world, the American example and American influence would become irrelevant. It was also feared that in such a world the integrity of the nation's institutions and the quality of its domestic life would be seriously jeopardized.

The profound revolution in American foreign policy that attended the defeat of the Axis powers and the containment of the Soviet Union was thus a necessary revolution; largely the same may be said of the creation of the national security state that was its inevitable accompaniment. Under the shield provided by American military power, and by virtue of enlightened measures of economic statesmanship, the peoples of Europe and Northeast Asia gave play to the creative and constructive impulses that had decayed under the shadow of war. The economic miracle that resulted was accompanied by a political miracle as Europe and

200   Japan purged their internal demons and built constitutional democracies that offered their citizens just and stable frameworks of
government unknown to the lost generation. This accomplishment, which entailed a vast enlargement of the sphere of ordered
liberty, represented the real greatness of the postwar American
imperium.

The renovation of American policy today must surely take
account of this accomplishment. It would be foolish to surrender
the advantages of alliances with Western Europe and Japan because they represent commitments against which the founders
warned. Though the United States might reasonably look forward
to the day when a federated Europe assumes sole responsibility for
its own defense, that day has not yet arrived. It is even more
distant in the case of Japan. In both cases, the key problem
remains the nuclear status of the defeated states of World War II.
For the foreseeable future, we must reckon with the possibility that
an American withdrawal from either alliance would create pressures not otherwise arising for Germany and Japan to acquire
nuclear weapons, a development there is no reason to encourage.
A nuclear Germany and Japan would not only awaken old fears in
Europe and east Asia; the instability that might follow such a
portentous move might also threaten the stability of the global
trading system. In the case of Japan, it might very well foster a
degree of antagonism in the American-Japanese relationship that,
added to the elements of discord now existing, could endanger the
security of both countries.

Then, too, a decision to acquire nuclear weapons by Germany and Japan would inevitably affect antiproliferation efforts
generally. That decision, however acquiesced in by the other
nuclear powers, would set a precedent that could not but gravely
prejudice such efforts. The present international system may remain one marked by great inequalities, but it is also one committed as never before to the principle of equality. To encourage in the
cases of Germany and Japan what is forbidden in the cases of other,
though far less advantaged, aspirants to nuclear status would surely
go far in stripping an antiproliferation regime of such legitimacy as
it might possess. Under the circumstances, the course of wisdom

would seem to dictate the retention of the alliances with Western Europe and Japan, a central part of which has always been the American nuclear guarantee, while also adjusting defense policy to reflect the fact that the security of this community of the advanced industrialized democracies is achievable at far less cost than was paid during the years of the cold war. *

The case for preserving as much continuity in the Western alliance as changed circumstances permit reflects the assumption that the nations comprising these alliances continue to embody the nation's principal interests in the world. It also reflects the assumption that the periphery of American policy during the cold war remains the periphery in the wake of the cold war. The latter

---

* It may of course be argued that Japan and Germany cannot be great powers without nuclear weapons, that the disparity between their economic status and their military status is an anomaly that cannot be sustained indefinitely, and that eventually they must move to surmount this disparity. Under current circumstances, however, their motives for taking such a step do not appear strong. The reality in Europe and Asia today is not only the emergence of a powerful Germany and Japan but of states that, so long as they eschew the old and disastrous ways, are likely to have few constraints placed on their freedom. The acquisition of nuclear weapons would seriously handicap the pursuit of an ever larger economic and political role. Nor is it likely that Germany and Japan will go nuclear in response to a precipitating event that suddenly reveals a threat to security only nuclear weapons can effectively counter. In the past, the existence of such a threat posed by the Soviet Union did not prompt either power to seek an independent nuclear capability, despite persistent fears over the credibility of the American deterrent. With the end of the cold war, there is less reason today to question the credibility of the American nuclear deterrent than there has been in decades.

A much more likely route to a nuclear capability would be a decision made in response to a lengthy train of events during which national pride and self-respect have been wounded once too often. In the case of both countries, it is the United States that is capable of inflicting the gravest of such wounds. The gulf war afforded the first object lesson of a process that might well result in the nuclear armament of the defeated states of World War II. If Germany and Japan are to pay the military bills of the new world order and to suffer slights to their national dignity while doing so, to have little or no say in how the new world order is implemented, the response might be to acquire nuclear weapons. That response, in turn, would lead in all likelihood to a policy disposition incompatible with the maintenance of the alliance structure over which America has presided since the immediate post–World War II years.

202   assumption, however, has been challenged today by a vision that, if put into practice, would extend an American security guarantee to virtually the entire world. In pursuit of this vision of a new world order, the nation is to exercise a police power which confers the right to prevent states of the developing world from acquiring certain weapons, and which imposes the duty to guarantee the territorial integrity of the members of the international community. In pursuit of this vision we are to maintain powerful interventionary forces capable of instantly responding, and on a large scale if need be, to "multiple contingencies" on the periphery.

Although the vision of a new world order has been set forth as novel, it is in fact the latest manifestation of an outlook that found periodic expression during the decades of the contest with the Soviet Union. Then, it took the form of global containment which proclaimed the need to resist the expansion of Soviet power and influence, if necessary by force, wherever and however this expansion occurred. Global containment rested on the assumptions that in the contest between the Soviet Union and the United States lines could not be drawn; that we could not pick and choose those places where we had to contain Soviet expansion; that the periphery if neglected would soon become the center; and that when engaged in a conflict for global stakes, what appeared as a marginal interest was all too often invested with critical significance, for almost any challenge was likely to be seen by the adversary making the challenge and by third parties as a test of one's will.

Global containment led us into Vietnam, just as global containment kept us there long after the dangers attending the intervention had become apparent. Vietnam taught, or should have taught, the difficulty of applying the precepts of a conventional—and conservative—statecraft to the policy of global containment, for the prudence of the one is not the prudence of the other. Whether global containment was supported by geopolitical considerations or justified on ideological grounds—and it was compatible with either rationale—the result was the same. In either case, the reconciliation of interest and power proved elusive. Whereas power is always limited, the interest informing global containment was not. The ever threatening disparity between interest and power could not be bridged simply by an act of will—a will ever triumphant because of the interest or purpose it reflected. Eventually, as in the case of Vietnam, the conviction of an ever triumphant will was bound to overtax power and to betray interest.

Yet what once proved elusive no longer appears so. What once constrained our actions no longer appears to do so. In the wake of the cold war and the gulf war, American military power seems virtually unlimited, particularly with respect to the vast region of the developing world. The gulf war provided a vivid demonstration of the effectiveness of this power, and at only a modest cost. In these novel and unexpected circumstances, an interest possessing the scope of global containment may readily take on an attractiveness it would never have otherwise possessed. That this interest does not respond to the reasonable security requirements of the nation, that it does not even have the security justification global containment could legitimately claim, need not prove decisive for its prospects. Given the protean character of security, policies justified in its name may usually be given a semblance of plausibility. Besides, for those who are not satisfied with justifying the use of American power in terms of an international order that is equated with the nation's security, there is always the additional justification seemingly provided by purpose. Although the world has been made safer for democracy than at any time in this century, the argument can be and is put forth that it may be made still safer.

Given the favorable power circumstances in which the Bush administration would today pursue its vision of world order, a policy that is the functional equivalent of global containment for the post–cold war world has evident attractions. The nation has succumbed to these attractions before, at times to its bitter regret. The experience we have had with the developing world stands in sharp contrast to our experience with Europe and Japan. In the developing world vast disparities in power and in institutional forms have made impossible what was achieved in our relations with the advanced industrialized democracies, an ethic of mutual cooperation and a sense of comity. Whereas our relations with the

204   nations that formed the core of American postwar policy often brought out what was very nearly the best in us, our relations with the nations that formed the periphery of American policy often evoked what was close to the worst in us. Nor is there reason to believe that this experience will now change for the better. If anything, it is likely that, with the end of the cold war, it will grow still worse now that a principal incentive for restrained behavior on our part has been removed. When the opportunity provided by the end of the cold war is joined with the ostensible lesson of the gulf war, the result could well be a greater disposition to intervene in the developing world. That disposition, if acted upon, will prove as corrupting to the nation in the future as it has proven in the past.

★   ★   ★

These strictures against intervention in the periphery would be worth observing even if the United States enjoyed the kind of economic surpluses it once did, but those surpluses are a thing of the past. It is true that military spending is not the sole cause of the inability of the nation to live within its means; it is equally apparent, however, that this inability reflects profound structural causes that pose a serious, long-term threat to the well-being of Americans and to the stability of the world financial system. The continuing budget deficits represent a profound disorder within the American body politic, a fundamental disequilibrium between the wants of the people and their willingness to sustain the sacrifices necessary to secure those wants. As a consequence of this disorder, interest payments on the debt have been far and away the most explosive expenditure of government in the 1980s. Although there is no reason to suppose that the needs of future generations will be any less exigent than our own, we persist in a policy of financial profligacy that can be defended only on this assumption.

Next to the existence of a formidable national security establishment itself, no feature of our current position would have so astonished and mortified the statesmen of the late eighteenth and nineteenth centuries as this propensity, in a period of peace, to run ceaselessly into debt. That propensity, unless reversed, will lead,

sooner or later, to "great and convulsive revolutions of empire"[2]— **205**
revolutions that will adversely affect the core, as opposed to the
peripheral, interests of the nation. Under the circumstances, it
seems evident that military expenditures should meet the test of
necessity. If current military expenditures were subjected to a rule
in which both wars and the preparation for war were considered as
something to be paid out of current expenditures, so that avarice
might calculate the expenses of ambition, we would be in a far
better position to judge the weight of these necessities and the
value of these ambitions.

★   ★   ★

There is no reason today why a skepticism about military
intervention may not coexist with a stance that is internationalist
in other respects—one that recognizes the necessity of cooperation among the great representative democracies to preserve an
open global trading system and to contend with a host of other
functional problems. At the same time, however, and more dis-
turbingly, there is also no reason to suppose that an increasingly
nationalistic public, resolutely opposed to foreign aid and increasingly attracted by protectionism, will also be opposed to the use of
American military power. As long as interventions, on the model
of the gulf war, promise to be relatively painless in blood and
treasure, they might well enjoy substantial support from a public
that is otherwise growing more isolationist.

Concern over the fate of free institutions and the conditions
of world order will certainly continue to inform the American
approach to foreign policy. Given the role that order and liberty
have always played in reflections on the American purpose, such
concern is both inevitable and appropriate. In pursuit of this
concern, however, military power has assumed a role that is excessive in the light of traditional conceptions of the national purpose.
In making force the primary basis of our power and influence in the
world we risk betraying the distinctive purpose of America. The
progressive expansion of the ends on behalf of which force is
threatened or employed, whether on behalf of world order, as with

206   Bush, or the extension of freedom, as with Reagan, is a corruption
of the original understanding.

This disproportionate emphasis on military power is nowhere
more apparent than in the gross disparity between the amount the
nation spends on "defense" and the good work it performs to assist
nations struggling to make the transition to representative democracy and market systems. Even with the reduction in military
forces planned by the Bush administration, the national defense
budget authority the administration plans to request between
fiscal 1992 and 1996 (in 1992 dollars) amounts to $1,361.7
billion.[3] The economic aid that might make the most significant
contribution to the establishment and growth of free institutions,
however, is scrutinized by the public with near fanatical intensity.
Billions for defense, it tells the politicians, not one cent for
philanthropy. The public consents to these large military expenditures because it is persuaded that they are necessary for America's
security, when in fact the greater part is necessary only if it is
thought that the nation ought to undertake a vast philanthropic
enterprise to order the world through its military power. Insofar as
there is an obligation to engage in such philanthropy, however, it
might be far better expressed by assisting in the development of the
institutions of civil society among those peoples who have given
clear evidence of a willingness to make the transition.

That such an opportunity presents itself today is clear. The
waves of democratization that have swept across Eastern Europe,
the Soviet Union, and Latin America offer a chance, which may
prove fleeting, to solidify and stabilize free institutions through
peaceful measures.[4] Sadly, however, the nation appears unwilling
to make the tangible commitments of resources that would assist in
the reconstruction of these economies and thus support their
experiments in freedom. Given the scale of our own domestic
problems, such an attitude is surely understandable, even if regrettable. Less understandable, and even harder to justify, is the
belief that our new calling, under the novel circumstances created
by the end of the cold war, is to create a universal alliance against
aggression, enforced by American military power. To refuse both
tasks, under the exigent pressures of domestic crisis, would at least

give consistency to the rejection of internationalism. But to refuse **207**
the one, while embracing the other, can only be deplored.

The outlook that informs American foreign policy today, of
which Bush's vision of a new world order is a vivid expression,
assumes that aggression, wherever it might occur, is a disease to
which this nation must supply the antidote. A more detached view
would allow us to see that aggression normally generates powerful
opposing forces among those most immediately threatened by it.
Rare are the occasions in which a hegemonic power, in the manner
of Napoleon or Hitler, either aspires to or has a chance of realizing
the mastery of the state system. It is not generally true, as Harry
Truman said in 1951, that "if history has taught us anything, it is
that aggression anywhere in the world is a threat to peace everywhere in the world." [5] It is not generally true, as George Bush said
in 1990, that "every act of aggression unpunished . . . strengthens the forces of chaos and lawlessness that, ultimately, threaten
us all." [6] This kind of universalism is the bane of American foreign
policy in the twentieth century. If history has taught us anything,
it is precisely the contrary of the lesson drawn by those who urge us
to be the world's policeman. It is that peace is normally divisible
and that conflicts, whatever their origin, are normally of merely
local or regional significance. To convert a lesson drawn from
America's experience with the totalitarian great powers of this
century into a general rule applicable to smaller powers is an
altogether misleading basis of national security policy.

The rejection of a *Pax Universalis* does not require a return to
the rule of nonentanglement characteristic of nineteenth century
American diplomacy. It need not, in particular, entail a withdrawal from the security commitments with which the United
States encumbered itself during the cold war. Power does entail
responsibility. If the architects of the new world order, who have
often recurred to this maxim, have forgotten that one of these
responsibilities is a restrained and moderate attitude toward the
use of force, the maxim does nevertheless contain an important
truth.

The principal aim of American security policy today ought to
be a devolution of substantial responsibilities to alliance partners,

208   together with the retention of existing security commitments. Such a devolution of power was presumably a principal aim of American policy during much of the cold war. If it was deemed a sensible aspiration in the midst of a hegemonial conflict, it is difficult to see why it should be rejected today. The expectation of American policy would be that the states with which we have security commitments are not thereby relieved of the obligation to assume primary responsibility for their own defense. Such an aim would make possible a far more substantial reduction in defense expenditures than that contemplated by the Bush administration, but it would not gratuitously introduce elements of instability where stability now prevails.

Though the Bush administration has not repudiated the principle of devolution in theory, its attitude in practice has been far more ambivalent. During the Iraqi crisis, it made little effort to find even a partial substitute for American power in the capabilities of regional states. It has looked with skepticism and a thinly veiled disapproval on the formation of a joint Franco-German force within the confines of the Western European Union, seeing such a force as a threat to American predominance in NATO. In its plans for rapidly deployable forces, there is little hint of the desirability of introducing policies, on the model of the Nixon Doctrine, that have as their aim either a division of labor or a devolution of responsibility. A *Pax Universalis*, after all, could hardly be sustained on the basis of such modest aspirations.

★   ★   ★

It is not only the traditional attitude toward world order and American security that might be partially rehabilitated in current circumstances, but the nation's traditional outlook toward the spread of free institutions. Such a renovation of American policy would represent a difficult undertaking; there is today a widespread consensus that it is our duty to demand of foreign states far-reaching reforms in their domestic policy on behalf of human rights. The main difference arises over the means by which this end may be pursued. A coup in Haiti, repression in China, apartheid in South Africa, communism in Cuba—all call forth the impulse to punish, whether that punishment takes the form of economic sanctions, the withholding (or withdrawal) of diplomatic recognition, or even, in some circumstances, the use of force. This impulse is not the exclusive possession of either the Right or Left in this country. On several occasions, the Democrats have outbid the Republicans in their denunciations of wrongdoing by foreign states, though they have shied away from forcible measures. Just as the proponents of the new world order have appropriated the Hamiltonian tradition of military preparedness and corrupted it through the lavish expansion (or universalization) of the American security frontier, so the proponents of nonforcible sanctions on behalf of human rights have also corrupted the Jeffersonian tradition of peaceable coercion. Although Jefferson did look forward to the subversive effects that the example of free institutions would have on other peoples, he never linked economic sanctions and nonrecognition by them to changes in the internal character of foreign states. That link was first made by Woodrow Wilson.

A policy of economic sanctions on behalf of human rights today carries four main dangers. First, the infliction of severe economic deprivation on other states may give rise to widespread suffering, objectionable on humanitarian grounds particularly when resorted to with such readiness by the rich against the poor. Second, such suffering hardly seems commensurate with the benefits gained in promoting liberalization.* Third, such policies may

---

* Commercial contacts with repressive states, such as China and South Africa, do encourage liberalizing tendencies. Such tendencies are seldom powerful enough to sweep everything before them, but then neither are punitive economic sanctions. Though each case is sufficiently different that it is difficult to make generalizations, three general considerations may be urged on behalf of the maintenance of commercial contacts even with repressive states. One is that such contacts help build the foundations of a civil society in preparation for the day when the old regime falls apart or feels impelled to moderate its repressive conduct. A second is that such contacts increase the likelihood of peaceful as opposed to revolutionary change. The latter seldom issues in a civil society, even if the apparatus of repressive power is swept away in violent upheaval. A third is that such contacts normally give dissident groups a window on the world that a severing of such ties might otherwise deny them.

210   lead to consequences we are unwilling to address, as it did in 1991 when intervention in Haiti produced refugees the administration had no intention of receiving (until temporarily forced to do so by a federal court). Finally, the demand that foreign states conform to a liberal or democratic standard may ultimately lead to war if nonforcible methods fail. These considerations may not justify in all cases a return to the rules governing recognition and intervention in the internal affairs of other states characteristic of nineteenth century American diplomacy; they do, however, justify a far more skeptical attitude toward the now well-nigh irresistible call for economic sanctions on behalf of liberty.

The traditional outlook was admittedly austere. It accorded recognition to foreign governments if they met the test of effectiveness and adhered to their international obligations. It refrained from intervention in the internal affairs of other states. It assumed an obligation to teach by example, thus directing primary attention to reforming the ills of American society while aiming for the "high, plain, yet dizzy ground that separates influence from intervention."[7] It was universalist in the sense that it assumed that the philosophical assumptions underlying the institutions of civil freedom were in principle open to all humanity, if humanity would have the wit to see them. But it went not abroad, in search of monsters to destroy. It understood that to do so would entail an insensible change in the fundamental maxims of American policy "from *liberty* to *force*."[8]

Our recent experience has not refuted the wisdom embodied in this traditional outlook. It was the example of a prosperous and free Western civilization, built on the basis of principles recognizably American, that ensured the doom of communism. A patient policy of military containment played a very important role in the success of this policy, but the efficient cause lay elsewhere, in the power of example. Silenced for a time by military power, that example proved in the end to be "elastic, irrepressible, and invulnerable to the weapons of ordinary warfare."[9]

The old method, however, no longer has the appeal it once did. The irony of the present moment is that, while our own maxims are in danger of changing from liberty to force, free institutions have captured the imagination of peoples throughout **211** the world. We may indeed deceive ourselves in thinking that this development augurs the "end of history"—understood as the permanent ascendancy of liberal institutions and as the endpoint of mankind's ideological evolution—but there is little doubt that the ideas of representative democracy and of the system of natural liberty do have an extraordinary appeal and power in the world today. If seen from the perspective of the traditional conception of the American purpose, such a development must appear profoundly gratifying. Yet we are willing to offer very little to solidify this auspicious development, nor have we seen it as an opportunity to rid the nation of the real and imagined necessities acted upon during fifty years of struggle with the totalitarian powers. Instead, the end of the cold war, which both vindicated the traditional American purpose and sharply diminished threats to American security, is seen as an opportunity to create a putative universal alliance against aggression, enforced by American military power.

This enterprise, so often justified as a vindication of the American purpose, represents its betrayal. It prefigures, in fact, the end of American history. For though we may be assured that history as such will never end, particular histories end all the time. The momentary achievements of men and nations may live on in memory for a time, but in the normal course of events they are forgotten or survive only as objects of curiosity to antiquarians. The proud boast of American statecraft was once that we were different in this respect, that we would not forget the admonitions of the Founding Fathers and their successors, nor suffer the basic principles of the American experiment to undergo corruption. American history will come to an end when these sentiments no longer animate our political life.

N O T E S

INTRODUCTION

1. Charles Krauthammer, "The Unipolar Moment," *Foreign Affairs: America and the World 1990/91*, 70, no. 1, p. 24.
2. Paul Kennedy, "A Declining Empire Goes to War," *The Wall Street Journal*, January 24, 1991.

CHAPTER 2

1. President Bush, "Toward a New World Order," Address before a joint session of Congress, September 11, 1990, *U.S. Department of State Dispatch* 1, no. 3 (September 17, 1990), pp. 91–94.
2. President Bush, "State of the Union Address," January 29, 1991, *Dispatch* 2, no. 5 (February 4, 1991), pp. 65–67.
3. President Bush, "Address to Joint Session of Congress," *Dispatch* 2, no. 7 (March 7, 1991), p. 162.
4. Message of President Harry Truman to Congress, March 12, 1947. *A Decade of American Foreign Policy, Basic Documents 1941–49*. Senate Committee on Foreign Relations, Washington, D.C.: G.P.O., 1950), p. 1256.
5. Statement by President Bush, January 3, 1991, "Persian Gulf Crisis: Going the Extra Mile for Peace," *Dispatch* 2, no. 1, p. 1.
6. President Bush, "State of the Union," February 4, 1991, *Dispatch* 2, no. 5, p. 67.

CHAPTER 3

1. "Korean Problems," Address by Secretary Dulles before the American Legion, St. Louis, Missouri. *Department of State Bulletin* XXIX, September 2, 1953, p. 339

2. Statement by Robert H. Jackson, Chief Counsel for the United States in the **213** Prosecution of Axis War Criminals, August 8, 1945, *Department of State Bulletin* XIII, p. 228.
3. Cited in Walter Millis, with Harvey C. Mansfield and Harold Stein, *Arms and the State: Civil-Military Elements in National Policy* (New York: The Twentieth Century Fund, 1958), p. 272.
4. Statement by Secretary of State Dean Acheson, June 26, 1951, House Committee on Foreign Affairs, *Hearings, Mutual Security Program*, 82nd Congress, 1st Session, p. 25.

CHAPTER 4

1. President Wilson, "Address at Cheyenne," September 24, 1919, *The Papers of Woodrow Wilson*, Arthur S. Link et al., eds. (Princeton: Princeton University Press, 1990), vol. 63, p. 469.
2. H.A. Smith, *The Crisis in the Law of Nations* (London: Stevens, 1947), p. 90.
3. President Franklin Roosevelt, Address to Congress, March 1, 1945, *The Public Papers and Addresses of Franklin D. Roosevelt*, Samuel I. Rosenman, ed. (New York: Harper & Brothers, 1950), vol. 13, p. 586.
4. Senate Committee on Foreign Relations Hearings, *North Atlantic Treaty*, 81st Congress, 1st Session, Pt. I, p. 143.
5. Ibid., pp. 334–37.

CHAPTER 5

1. UN Resolution 678, which authorized the use of force, was passed on November 29, 1990. For the text of UN resolutions on the gulf crisis, see Micah L. Sifry and Christopher Cerf, eds., *The Gulf War Reader: History, Documents, Opinions* (New York: Times Books, 1991).
2. Quoted in Michael Dobbs and Rick Atkinson, "Soviets Say Iraq's Response 'Positive'; Bush Calls Pullout Plan Unacceptable," *The Washington Post*, February 22, 1991.
3. See Lawrence Korb, "Padding The Gulf War Bill," *The New York Times*, April 4, 1991.
4. Judith Miller, "Displaced in the Gulf War: 5 Million Refugees," *The New York Times*, June 16, 1991.

CHAPTER 6

1. President Bush, "Toward a New World Order," Address before a joint session of Congress, September 11, 1990, *U.S. Department of State Dispatch* 1, no. 3, (September 17, 1990), p. 92.

214

2. President Bush, "Remarks at a Fundraising Luncheon for Rep. Bill Grant," September 6, 1990, *Weekly Compilation of Presidential Documents* 26, no. 36, p. 1331.

3. Secretary of State James Baker, "Why America Is in the Gulf," Address before the Los Angeles World Affairs Council, October 29, 1990, *Dispatch* 1, no. 10, p. 235.

4. President Bush, "Operation Desert Storm Launched," January 16, 1991, *Dispatch* 2, no. 3, p. 37.

5. Secretary Baker, "Isolation Strategy Toward Iraq," Statement before the Senate Foreign Relations Committee, October 17, 1990, *Dispatch* 1, no. 8, p. 206.

6. Secretary Baker, "America's Stake in the Persian Gulf," Statement before the House Foreign Affairs Committee, September 4, 1990, *Dispatch* 1, no. 2, p. 69.

7. President Bush, "Operation Desert Storm Launched," January 16, 1991, *Dispatch* 2, no. 3, p. 37.

8. Ibid.

9. President Bush, "State of the Union," January 29, 1991, *Dispatch* 2, no. 5, p. 66.

10. President Bush, "Operation Desert Storm Launched," January 16, 1991, *Dispatch* 2, no. 3, p. 37.

11. Henry A. Kissinger, Testimony before the Senate Armed Services Committee, November 28, 1990. On November 12, 1990, *The New York Times* reported that a senior administration official had said "that Arab resentment against the American military presence might grow if the U.S. keeps large numbers of troops in Saudi Arabia for a prolonged period. The official also expressed concern that American fighting men might lose their edge and that the multinational coalition arrayed against Iraq might unravel if the crisis remained unresolved for an extended period." See Michael R. Gordon, "Nunn, Citing 'Rush' to War, Assails Decision to Drop Troop Rotation Plan." *The New York Times*, November 12, 1990.

12. President Bush to Saddam Hussein, January 5, 1991, *Dispatch* 2, no. 2, p. 25.

CHAPTER 7

1. President Bush, "Remarks to Community Members at Fort Stewart, Georgia," February 1, 1991, *Weekly Compilation of Presidential Documents* 27, no. 6, p. 113.

2. See Michael R. Gordon, "Baker Cites 2 Aims: Kuwait and Captives," *The New York Times*, December 3, 1990.

3. Andrew Rosenthal, "U.S. Said to Want Sanctions Kept After a Pullout," *The New York Times*, December 14, 1990.

4. See, for instance, David Hoffman, "Two Stiff Necks That Would Not Bend: Misjudgments Pushed Bush and Hussein into a Corner," *The Washington Post National Weekly Edition*, January 21–27, 1991, p. 19.

5. Statement by President Bush, January 3, 1991, "Persian Gulf Crisis: Going **215** the Extra Mile for Peace," *Dispatch* 2, no. 1, p. 1.

6. Senator Mitchell, *Congressional Record*, S 101, January 10, 1991.

CHAPTER 8

1. The policy of punitive containment sketched out here is similar in many, but not all, respects to that set forth, under the name of "punitive deterrence," by Zbigniew Brzezinski. See his "Patience in the Persian Gulf, Not War," *The New York Times*, October 7, 1990; and "The True U.S. Interest in the Gulf," *The Washington Post*, August 16, 1990.

2. President Bush, "Remarks at the Arrival Ceremony in Helsinki, Finland," September 8, 1990, *Weekly Compilation of Presidential Documents* 26, no. 36, p. 1342.

3. In the congressional debate on the eve of war, Senator Daniel Patrick Moynihan recalled that, during his tenure as Ambassador to the United Nations, and on the occasion of the UN resolution equating Zionism with racism, the Kuwaitis had been "singularly nasty," "personally loathsome," and "conspicuously poisonous." *Congressional Record*, S 109, January 10, 1991.

4. See chapter 11, "Justice and the War," for a more extensive discussion of this question.

5. For an instructive commentary on the efficacy of the sanctions, see Kimberly Elliott, Gary Hufbauer, and Jeffrey Schott, "The Big Squeeze: Why the Sanctions on Iraq Will Work," *The Washington Post*, December 9, 1990.

6. "Excerpts from Bush's Statement on U.S. Defense of Saudis," *The New York Times*, August 9, 1990; "Excerpts from Bush's News Conference on the Iraqi Invasion of Kuwait," *The New York Times*, August 9, 1990.

7. R.W. Apple, Jr., "Bush Draws 'Line': He Rules Out an Invasion of Kuwait— Troops Take Up Positions," *The New York Times*, August 9, 1990.

CHAPTER 9

1. See Matthew Meselson, "The Myth of Chemical Superweapons," *The Bulletin of Atomic Scientists*, April 1991, pp. 12–15.

2. R. Jeffrey Smith, "Iraq's A-Arms Effort: Grim Lessons for the World," *The Washington Post*, August 11, 1991.

3. Ibid

4. See, for instance, Charles Krauthammer, "The Unipolar Moment," *Foreign Affairs: America and the World 1990/91*, pp. 30–32; and Alan Tonelson, "What is the National Interest?," *The Atlantic Monthly* 268, no. 1 (July 1991), p. 51.

5. See Thomas C. Schelling, *Arms and Influence* (New Haven: Yale University Press, 1966), for the classic exposition of this problem.

6. See "The Glaspie Transcript: Saddam Meets the U.S. Ambassador, July 25, 1990," in Michael L. Sifry and Christopher Cerf, eds., *The Gulf War Reader: History, Documents, Opinions* (New York: Times Books, 1991) p. 130.
7. Nora Boustany and Patrick E. Tyler, "U.S. Pursues Diplomatic Solution in Persian Gulf Crisis, Warns Iraq," *The Washington Post*, July 25, 1990.

CHAPTER 11

1. President Bush, "The Gulf: A World United Against Aggression," Opening Statement at a White House news conference, November 30, 1990, *Dispatch* 1, no. 14, p. 296.
2. See Dan Balz and Rick Atkinson, "Powell Vows to Isolate Iraqi Army and 'Kill It,'" *The Washington Post*, January 24, 1991; and George Bush to Saddam Hussein, January 5, 1991, *Dispatch* 2, no. 2, p. 25.

CHAPTER 12

1. The most persuasive case for the feasibility of establishing in Iraq "a demilitarized, genuinely secular, federated republic founded on working democratic institutions" was made by the expatriate Iraqi Kanan Makiya, writing under the pseudonym Samir al-Khalil, in "Iraq and Its Future," *The New York Review of Books*, April 11, 1991, pp. 10–14. On the feasibility of democratic constitutionalism in Iraq, see Laurie Mylroie, *The Future of Iraq* (Washington, D.C.: The Washington Institute for Near East Policy, 1991), Policy Paper no. 24; and Ahmad Chalabi, "Iraq: The Past as Prologue?" *Foreign Policy*, Summer 1991, no. 83, pp. 20–29.
2. See "On to the Elbe?" *The Wall Street Journal*, February 21, 1991.
3. William Safire, "Bush's Moral Crisis," *The New York Times*, April 1, 1991. "If we are too timid to impose democracy," Safire wrote, "we owe it to our sense of right and wrong to at least level the killing field."
4. See "Rest in Pieces," *The New Republic*, April 8, 1991.
5. Cited in Elizabeth Drew, "Letter From Washington," *The New Yorker*, May 7, 1991, p. 97.
6. Edward Mortimer, "Iraq: The Road Not Taken," *The New York Review of Books*, May 16, 1991, p. 3.

CHAPTER 13

1. President Bush, "Radio Address to United States Armed Forces Stationed in the Persian Gulf Region," March 2, 1991, *Weekly Compilation of Presidential Documents* 27, no. 10, p. 245.
2. President Bush, "Remarks at a Meeting of the American Legislative Exchange Council," March 1, 1991, *Weekly Compilation of Presidential Documents* 27, no. 9, p. 233.
3. Dante Fascell, quoted in David Shribman, "Victory in Gulf War Exorcises the Demons of the Vietnam Years," *The Wall Street Journal*, March 1, 1991.

4. "Excerpts from Bush's News Conference on Postwar Moves," *The New York* **217** *Times*, March 2, 1991.
5. R.W. Apple, Jr., "A Short, Persuasive Lesson in Warfare," *The New York Times*, March 3, 1991.
6. President Johnson, "Address at Johns Hopkins University: 'Peace Without Conquest,'" April 7, 1965, *Public Papers of the Presidents of the United States: Lyndon B. Johnson, 1965* (Washington, D.C.: G.P.O., 1966), I, p. 395.
7. Ibid.
8. Anthony H. Cordesman, "America's New Combat Culture," *The New York Times*, February 28, 1991.
9. "Excerpts from Interview with Commander of American Forces in Gulf," *The New York Times*, November 2, 1990.
10. John Bassett Moore, *International Law and Some Current Illusions* (New York: Macmillan, 1924), p. 24.

CHAPTER 15

1. Daniel Webster, "Speech on the Panama Mission," April 14, 1826, in Edward Everett, ed., *The Works of Daniel Webster* (Boston: Little, Brown & Co., 1851), III, p. 193.
2. Ibid.
3. Moses Coit Tyler, *The Literary History of the American Revolution, 1763–1783*, 2 vols. (New York: G.P. Putnam's, 1897), I, p. 221.
4. Letters of Helvidius, No. IV, *The Writings of James Madison*, Gaillard Hunt, ed. (New York: G.P. Putman's Sons, 1900–1910, 9 vols.) VI, p. 174.
5. James Madison, Eighth Annual Message, December 3, 1816, in James D. Richardson, ed., *A Compilation of the Messages and Papers of the Presidents, 1789–1897* (Washington, D.C.: G.P.O., 1896–99, 10 vols), I, p. 580.
6. Alexander Hamilton, "Defense of the Funding System," *The Papers of Alexander Hamilton*, Harold Syrett et al., eds. (New York: Columbia University Press, 1961–79, 26 vols.), XIX, p. 56; p. 90.
7. Thomas Jefferson to John Dickinson, March 6, 1801, in Merrill Peterson, ed., *Thomas Jefferson: Writings* (New York: Library of America, 1984), p. 1084.
8. Alexander Hamilton, James Madison, and John Jay, *The Federalist Papers*, Clinton Rossiter, ed. (New York: New American Library, 1961), No. 1, p. 33.
9. "Peace with Mexico," [1847], Henry Adams, ed., *The Writings of Albert Gallatin* (Philadelphia: J.B. Lippincott and Co., 1960), III, p. 582.
10. Jefferson to Thomas Cooper, Nov. 29, 1802, in Paul Leicester Ford, ed., *The Writings of Thomas Jefferson* (New York: G.P. Putman's Sons, 1892–99, 10 vols.), VIII, p. 177.
11. Jefferson to Monroe, June 11, 1823, in ibid., X, p. 256.
12. Jefferson to Adams, May 17, 1818, in ibid., X, p. 107.
13. Daniel Webster, "Eulogy on Washington," February 22, 1832, in B.F. Tefft, ed., *The Speeches of Daniel Webster* (Philadelphia: Porter & Coates, 1854), pp. 251–52.

218

14. Daniel Webster, "The Greek Revolution," January 19, 1824, in Tefft, ed., *Speeches*, p. 134.

15. ————, January 12, 1852, in John Bassett Moore, ed., *A Digest of International Law* (Washington, D.C.: G.P.O., 1906, 8 vols.), VI, p. 16.

16. John Quincy Adams, *An Address Delivered at the Request of a Committee of the Citizens of Washington, on the Occasion of Reading the Declaration of Independence* (Washington, D.C.: Davis and Force, 1821), p. 29.

17. President Washington, "Farewell Address," September 17, 1796, in Richardson, ed., *Messages and Papers of the Presidents*, I, p. 222.

18. James Monroe, "Seventh Annual Message," December 2, 1823, in Richardson, ed., *Messages and Papers of the Presidents*, II, p. 218.

19. Henry Wheaton, *Elements of International Law: The Literal Reproduction of the Edition of 1866 by Richard Henry Dana, Jr.*, George Grafton Wilson, ed., (Oxford: Clarendon Press, 1936), p. 93n.

CHAPTER 16

1. Philip Jessup, *Elihu Root* (New York: Dodd, Mead & Co., 1938, 2 vols.), I, pp. 404–405.

2. Richard Olney, "Growth of Our Foreign Policy," *The Atlantic Monthly*, March 1900, p. 290.

3. Diary of Colonel Edward Mandell House, August 30, 1914, quoted in *The Papers of Woodrow Wilson*, Arthur S. Link et al., eds. (Princeton: Princeton University Press, 1966–, 64 vols. to date), III, p. 462.

4. Roland N. Stromberg, *Collective Security and American Foreign Policy: From the League of Nations to NATO* (New York: Praeger, 1963), p. 37.

5. Quoted in ibid., p. 33.

6. President Coolidge, Message to Congress, December 7, 1926, *Papers Relating to the Foreign Relations of the United States, 1926* (Washington, D.C.: G.P.O., 1941, 2 vols.), I, xxvi.

7. Walter Lippmann, *U.S Foreign Policy: Shield of the Republic* (Boston: Little Brown and Co., 1943), p. 92.

CHAPTER 20

1. William H. Seward, *Life and Public Services of John Quincy Adams* (Port Washington, N.Y.: Kennikat Press, 1971 [1849]), p. 360.

2. Alexander Hamilton, "Second Report on the Public Credit," January 20, 1795, *Papers on Public Credit, Commerce, and Finance*, Samuel McKee, Jr., and J. Harview Williams, eds. (Indianapolis: Bobbs-Merrill, 1957), p. 151.

3. See William W. Kaufmann and John D. Steinbruner, *Decisions for Defense: Prospects for a New Order* (Washington, D.C.: The Brookings Institution, 1991), pp. 37–38.

4. See James Schlesinger, "New Instabilities, New Priorities," *Foreign Policy*, **219** No. 85 (Winter, 1991–92), pp. 3–24. Schlesinger recommends that priority in reconstruction aid be given to Eastern Europe.
5. Address of April 11, 1951, excerpted in Thomas G. Paterson, ed., *Major Problems in American Foreign Policy, Vol. II: Since 1914* (Lexington, Mass.: D.C. Heath, 1989), p. 408.
6. President Bush, "Remarks at a Fundraising Luncheon for Rep. Bill Grant, Sept. 6, 1990, *Weekly Compilation of Presidential Documents* 26, no. 36, p. 1331.
7. Rufus Choate, "A Discourse Commemorative of Daniel Webster," July 27, 1853, *The Works of Rufus Choate*, Samuel Gilman Brown, ed. (Boston: Little, Brown and Co., 1862, 2 vols.), I, p. 520.
8. John Quincy Adams, *An Address Delivered at the Request of a Committee of the Citizens of Washington, on the Occasion of Reading the Declaration of Independence* (Washington, D.C.: Davis and Force, 1821), p. 29.
9. Daniel Webster, "The Greek Revolution," January 19, 1824, in B.F. Tefft, ed., *The Speeches of Daniel Webster* (Philadelphia: Porter & Coates, 1854), p. 134.

INDEX